TREBOR HEALEY

SWEET SON OF PAN

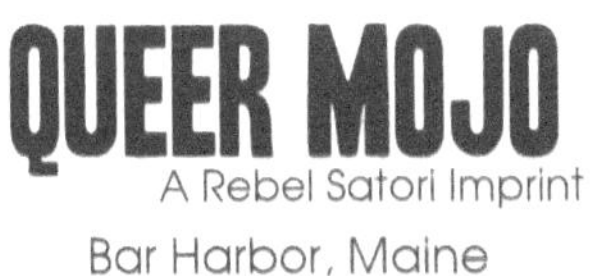

QUEER MOJO
A Rebel Satori Imprint
Bar Harbor, Maine

REBEL SATORI PRESS
P.O. Box 363
Hulls Cove, ME 04644
www.rebelsatori.com

Cover art by Joel Singer
Author photograph by Martin Cox
Cover/book design by Sven Davisson/Rebel Satori Press

ISBN: 978-1-60864-034-8

Library of Congress Cataloging-in-Publication Data

Healey, Trebor, 1962-
  Sweet son of Pan / Trebor Healey.
    p. cm.
    Originally published: San Francisco, CA: Suspect Thoughts Press, 2006.
  ISBN 978-1-60864-034-8 (pbk.)
1. Gay men--Poetry. I. Title.
 PS3608.E24S94 2010
  811'.6--dc22
                                        2010029520

ACKNOWLEDGMENTS

I wish to thank those who offered a ready ear for my work over the years, and especially those who encouraged me and helped me along in all the innumerable ways—financial, spiritual, inspirational and otherwise—that eventually led to this collection: the late Ernest Posey, Robert Hall, Jerry Thompson, the late Charles Swarengin, Larry Ackerman, Chuck Hawley, the late David Brown, Frank Shawl, Antler, Gerardo Perez, Sera Sacks, Isaac Cruz, Jeff Robertson, Alex Nowik, Hank and Keith, Bill Donovan, Roger Corless, Otis Fennel, Stevee Postman, Paul Willis, Greg Herren, Felice Picano, Andy Smith, Benjamin Morrison, Stephen Reigns, Scott Bailey, Stuart Timmons, Joy Nicholson, Karl Woelz, Vytautus Pliura, Ron Libertus, Mark Misrok, Bill Smartt, Jon Ginoli, the late Vivekan Flint, Daniel Kopyc and Horehound Stillpoint.

I owe a great debt of gratitude to Lois Silverstein and Sparrow 13 Laughing Wand, who were early and influential teachers, and I also want to acknowledge some very special communities that celebrate the erotic and have nurtured the voice that sings in these pages: The Radical Faeries, the Gay Men's Spiritual Retreat, the Discovery Community, the Billy Club, 848 Community Space, Good Vibrations, and all the poets through the ages who were not afraid to sing the body electric.

And thanks as well to all the poets of San Francisco who are too numerous to name here, but who are part of a vital spoken word community that I have been fortunate to be a part of and that has nurtured my voice. Ali Liebegott, Michelle Tea, Michele C, Eli Coppola, David West, Bucky Sinister, Nancy Depper, Justin Chin, Merle Tofer, Marci Blackman, among others, fed me with their inspired words, which I digested and transformed in the crucible of my own little heart into these poems. Special thanks to Jennifer Joseph, M.I. Blue, Carol Queen, Jack Davis, Bill Brent, and Hank Hyena who provided numerous venues for erotic poetry in the early and mid-'90s. Thanks as well to those who continually publish my poetry: Larry-bob Roberts, Sven Davisson, Jaime Cortez, Winston Leyland, Matteo Bianchi, Ian Ayres, Michael Hathaway, and Gavin Geoffrey Dillard.

Finally, a profound appreciation for the original publishers of this collection, the inimitable Ian Philips and Greg Wharton of Suspect Thoughts Press, and the current publisher, Sven Davisson of Rebel Satori Press, without whom I would not have been able to share this work with so many.

Ultimately, I must thank Priapus and Pan, Cernunnos, and the great good fortune of being born queer and randy, without which these songs would never have been sung.

The following poems previously appeared in these reviews, journals, and anthologies, sometimes in slightly altered form: "Bubble," published in *Bend, Don't Shatter* (Soft Skull Press, 2004). "Busboy Sutra," published in *Ashe!* (www.ashejournal.com, 2003). "Cruising," published in *Tight* (Vol. 7, No. 1, 1996). "Denny," published in *Holy Titclamps* (Issue #12, Summer, 1993). "Dick Prayer," published in *Dingus* (Issue #2, Summer, 1994). "Elegy for the Castro," published in *Out in the Castro* (Leyland Publications, 2002). "Evolution of the Castro," published in *Out in the Castro* (Leyland Publications, 2002). "Faerie Gathering," published in *Sex Spoken Here* (Down There Press, 1998). "Fraternity," published in *Signs of Life* (Manic D Press, 1994) and *Fratsex* (Alyson, 2004). "How the Lion Got Its Roar," published in *Speed Demon* (Issue #9, Autumn, 1997). "Hustler," published in *Dingus* (Issue #2, Summer, 1994), *Evergreen Chronicles* (Vol. 10, Winter/Spring, 1995), *Bad Boy Book of Erotic Poetry* (Masquerade, 1995), *Black Sheets,* and *A Day for a Lay: A Century of Gay Poetry* (Barricade Books, 1999). "If Thich Nhat Hanh Was a Fag Like Me," published in *Queer Dharma* (Gay Sunshine Press, 1998). "Iowa," published in *Dingus* (Issue #1, Spring, 1994) and *Corpus* (Institute for Gay Men's Health, 2006). "Jesus Christ, St. Sebastian, Etc., Etc.," published in *Day for a Lay: A Century of Gay Poetry* (Barricade Books, 1999). "Jonas' Fiat," published in *Between the Cracks* (Daedalus, 1996). "Make My Boyfriend a Buddha," published in

Queer Dharma (Gay Sunshine Press, 1998). "Milarepa," published in *Lodestar Quarterly* (www.lodestarquarterly.com, 2003). "Milky Way," published in *Blank Gun Silencer.* "My Perfect Androgyne," published in *Chiron Review* (Vol. 12, No. 3, Autumn, 1993), *Billys News* (Vol. 1, No. 4, Summer, 1993), and *Beyond Definition* (Manic D Press, 1994). "A Nightclub South of Market," published in *Priapus* (2002). *"O* Nobly Born," published in *Queer Dharma* (Gay Sunshine Press, 1998). "Ode to Buddha," published in *Queer Dharma* (Gay Sunshine Press, 1998). "Ode to DJ," published in *Bend, Don't Shatter* (Soft Skull Press, 2004). "Ode to His Butt," published in *Cupid* (1997). "Our Lady of Fresh Produce," published in *Beyond Definition* (Manic D Press, 1994). "Our Lady of the Fine Torso," published in *Whispering Campaign* (Issue #6, Winter, 1994) and *Chiron Review* (Vol. 12, No. 3, Autumn, 1993). "Our Lady of the Showers," published in *RFD* (Vol. 24, No. 4, Issue 94, Summer, 1998) and *Chiron Review* (Issue #81, Winter, 2005). "Pan," published in *Van Gogh's Ear #5* (French Connection Press, 2006). "Paris, Texas," published in *Cokefish* (February, 1993) and *Billys News* (Vol. 1, No. 3, Spring, 1993). "Religion," published in *Dingus* (Issue #1, Spring, 1994) and *Sex Spoken Here* (Down There Press, 1998). "Sex and Death," published in *Eidos* and *Sex Spoken Here* (Down There Press, 1998). "A Strapping Lad," published in *Van Gogh's Ear* #5 (French Connection Press, 2006). "We Started Out Janitors," published in *Black Sheets, Bad Boy Book of Erotic Poetry* (Masquerade, 1995) and *A Day for a Lay: A Century of Gay Poetry* (Barricade Books, 1999).

it's
spring
and
        the

                        goat-footed

balloonMan   whistles
far
and
wee

e.e. cummings, "in Just"

CONTENTS

Psalms for Centaurs and Satyrs

L'Envoi, or, Pagan Benediction

FOREWORD

I had avowed to write no more about secular literature. But I had an epiphany: great secular work inevitably embraces the Mystic—as religious writings oft avoid it like a plague. William Blake, after all, preached the essential embracing of carnality from the pulpit of his pen. Shakespeare used the folly of man as a stepping-stone to transcendence. Mirabai and Rumi, two of the greatest mystic poets of all time, bring God into the bedroom, the Spirit as eternal Lover.

No great work is produced from the powers of mind—which is only capable of regurgitating and reproducing the "known." It is solely through intercourse with Spirit that genius is unleashed—this indeed is the creative force, or intuition, which is the voice of the soul. This is how God speaks to us, when we deign to listen, and is the only purpose of great art.

Any worthwhile artist will eventually come to the end of his pen to discover that there is no one there. From whence does the poem originate; and who is it that directs the ink? So it has been with the great physicists of the world—Heisenberg, Schröedinger, Planck, and of course Daddy Einstein—who have invariably discovered through the adept dissection of either microcosm or macrocosm that Mystery reigns at either end. To name the artisans who have discovered the Void beyond the pen or canvas would require the length of this book—pick any of those whom we call genius.

Pan, after all, is not a deity. Rather he is a halfling, the demigod, born of a divine/sacred dad and a mortal/profane mom, thusly walking the line between heaven and earth. The fearful question his authority; but those who duly surrender—we suppliants to his dreadful allure—are raised up to that demarcation which separates the gross from the etheric. The choice then is ours alone; but I know one thing: those who leap are those who have fully consummated their mortality.

As for Master Trebor, he is a ring-bearer, a torch carrier, the legitimate bastard son of an endless line of bastard sons howling in the wilderness—dating back through Lorca, Cavafy, Whitman, to Catullus, Strato, and beyond. For as long as man is commanded to roam these sacred woods, somewhere, from some lone hilltop, licentious yet austere, this voice will ever be heard to howl. And Trebor is just this wolf. Hear his voice and tremble.

—Gavin Geoffrey Dillard, "the Naked Poet"

PROLOGUE,
OR, FIRST INVOCATION TO PAN

SESTINA FOR PAN

Among the footprints, I spied the outline of a hoof
A crescent it was, a revelation of exposed bone
It made me wet my mouth, and across my lips I ran my
 tongue
Something unseen, but cloven and with a hint of horn
That day was warm, of the good summer days of seed
I heard then an almost imperceptible far-off sound of pipes

Closer came the song of those pipes
A trotting sound too, of horseshoe or of hoof
A scent of pollen, the wind full-blown with seed
I felt a stirring deep within my bone
A prodding sensation behind me too, as if from a horn
The taste of chestnut settled on my tongue

I tasted it, and once again across my parched lips I ran my
 tongue
The song inside me now, I was a part of the pipes
I felt inside me as well the horn
Upon my sternum now I felt the pressure of that hoof
And heard the rattling sound of 2 lucky shaken dice of bone
Which shattered as they were thrown, spilling wet and
 squirming seed

The scent intoxicating of that splattered seed
I longed to lap it up now with my tongue
Then I felt more of it flinging outward from my very own
 bone
Which pressed against another, playing in tandem, a sweet
 duet of pipes
And there were hairy shins above the hoof
Above the swollen, swinging testes, an immense horn

I pranced about cloven-hoofed and made room now for that
 horn
Dripping now, as it bobbed about, swollen and wet with seed
Spilling and making luscious boy-mud upon his hoof
Across my chest he ran his wanton, serpentine tongue
Our lust, a song now, deafening as Scottish pipes
Inside me, and I in him, the sacred bone

Hot flesh wrapped tight that hard, insistent bone
So deep within each other, our slimed and prodding horn

A seductive and relentless moan of pipes
A sudden blast and I am full of seed!
I lose control now of my salivating tongue
My legs above my head, where once was foot, I see anew a
    hoof

And so was I, a youth, baptized by pipes and tongue
Penetrated by bone, a fertile field for manly seed
A rider of horn, blest forever now with this cloven hoof

HYMNS to BOYS
NOT NAMED GANYMEDE

SAN GABRIEL VALLEY

When we jack off together
In his truck
It's like tabla drums
I kiss him and he tastes like orange blossoms
"Dude, it's just that tea I drank,"

Each vein strung up his cock
As if it were a great sitar
But to him it's an electric guitar
He's a bass player
Not a poet
"Dude, I'm fucking hard,"

His balls, in my hands like dice
Egyptians made the first out of bones
And so I think of death
As his semen
Grunts out of him
"Dude, I'm nutting,"

The goddess Nut
But he's never heard of her
Ganymede, Antinous, Whitman's soldier boys
I don't read books
"Dude man, I dig your cock—you hungry?"

Down the hill for Carl's Jr.
It drips off his chin
What am I doing here?
Yo Yo Ma is playing cello, believe it or not
"Dude, want a bite?"

I smile at him, shaking my head; I think he's beautiful

A STRAPPING LAD

When I was a boy
I dissected a GI Joe
The plastic parts—legs, arms, head, torso—
Were all held together by taut strings
Knotted just so it held together
In a sort of tensile flexibility
Like tendons
Bungee cords
A coiled spring
Strength under pressure

That's what strapping is
That's what he is
Taut
Like a cum-loaded slingshot
Every muscle in his body knotted
And leveraged
Off the fulcrum
Of his manroot
And the drowsy balls
That blow smoke rings of semen
Which his penis turns into napalm
A roused dragon shooting white jellied fire

Even his sleepy-lidded eyes
That quiet face
Duplicitous as a scrotum
A mask of peace
A Venus Flytrap
A trickster jaw
A snake of seduction and sudden conquest

He has the longest body
Biceps about the size of my shoes or the cones of sugar pines
Hands the size of oven mitts
Imagine them pulling his prick out of your ass
Like a tray of steaming hot fudge brownies

How corn-fed is his face
The ruddy cheeks
Are his asscheeks as white and blushing?
How I long to split them like an ax and fuck him until his
    sphincter coughs up semen

His tits are like big pink rivets
On the metal plate of his Roman armored chest
His belly, under its shirt, is as tight as a rubber playground
    ball
Springloaded with tension
Give me your vomit, boy
I'd like to watch him take an explosive dump
(It is thus through him that I have come to understand scat)
Beauty is the teacher, always

Every dawn I'd lie in his tub
To receive his copious morning piss
How heavy as he shakes it off, like a bag of potting soil in his
    big hands
And there are seeds to come
His stiff piece of firewood shoots them like spring buds
As the ax of his desire fells us both
And splatters me with milky joy
Making of the potting soil delicious mud
And causing me to beg for his morning scat as well

He would be overeager when he fucked
For he is young
And his penis has him more than he it
He'd likely force me into handstands
Crush my face into the mattress
Draw blood
With sighful, "sorry, dude"s

His cock's message is hurricane-like
It *must be* this way
I must weather the storm
Batten down the hatches
Take the hit
Holler through the hurricane of him
Hurricane "Andrew," "Mitch," "Hugo,"—whatever—I don't
    know his name

God, those biceps
How swollen must be his cock
If all his muscles could shoot, I'd drown
—And willingly
How many times fucked would satisfy me?
How unpleasant would he need to be for me to lose interest
Before he ruined me?

How merciless if he were kind and came to love me
How strange and sad
That I would find it intolerable
Such limitlessness
Pleasure would dissolve me
He'd be my death
He is death

And how beautiful that death sits here next to me now
Sipping coffee and looking cute
And fuckable
He's even got a weird straightboy fumbling "lithp"
Death does
He smiles politely when I stare
I smile back
Cherishing my coming death
Like a perfect lover
I want to call out to him:

"When?"

I SING THE DICK CROOKED

I sing the dick crooked
and the bent dick sings back to me
with the harmony of a boldly plucked guitar—
boing
Like a finger it motions me toward it:
Come on over here

A wild and gamey kinda cock,
it perks up like dogs' ears and tails
turns up its cockbelly like a puppy
It's the funnest kinda cock
banana-silly and slippery

Dog-legged like a fairway on a golf course
Bent like a 9-iron
And I'm the 1ˢᵗ hole, the 9ᵗʰ hole, the 18ᵗʰ hole

I'm a jock of such cock
on a bender of a ballgame
pitching and catching
When I free it from its batting cage,
it swoops up and out
like a foul ball

And the crowd cheers in my testicles as it rises

Oh wide-angled angler
like a fishing pole straining
like the way a rainbow trout contorts in bent-cock elegance
Like a fishhook
crooked dick waits for me with its queer bait
and I'm a willing fish
with my big asshole-mouth
I'll fight like a marlin
Just reel me in   to paradise
and the ecstasy of your quicksilver
liquid metal from that bent tempered steel

I run singing into the middle of oncoming traffic
inspiring the big rigs to jackknife across the slippery myriads
   of lanes
in bent dick benedictions
spilling their white hot chemicals all over the highway of my chest

I sing the dick crooked
And bent dick desires break into my heart with tire irons
wrench it open with a twang
rip off my hetero stereo
type
and all the old hetero tapes
silencing the mawing hunger of my ass
by ripping the speakers out of my doors
and singing instead inside me
with fine white noise

I sing the dick crooked
I praise the dick crooked
I run down Folsom Street like Gene Kelly
singing in the sticky rain from a thousand bent cocks
swinging off that crooked steel madness
like a streetlight pole

Oh, great scrotums that sail across the sky
and rainbows that bend over backwards to bear their boners
and show their bellies
Oh cornucopia kinda cock
of cumulonimbus cumspurts
drop your blessings on me
rain down on me
Sing to me

My gravitational lust for your boomerang blowjob
sings   come back   come back
come right here
Cum
Bless me with your white magic, warlock cock
Like good cock karma
you get back what you give
and I'm giving to crooked cock
getting my meathook payback

Oh, I could sing the dick crooked forever
follow that curve like centrifugal force
and orbit the abdomens of the bow-dicked boys
until the end of my crooked days
singing my crooked song
Singing my crooked bent dick love song

MARTIN LUTHER KING JR. BLVD.,
SOUTH CENTRAL L.A.

I have a dream too…
That young gangbangers
will pull up at stoplights
and lean their bare hips out of cars
to cum on their rivals windows
—or if they're rolled down
ejaculate upon the tongues of their enemies
who then cross themselves and mutter
Amen
For thine is the kingdom, the power, the glory

I have a dream that young Pakistani men
In London suburbs
Will pack knapsacks full of lube and condoms
Proceed to the nearest Tube station
Drop their drawers
And fuck young English boys
In subway cars—
Who needs paradise in the hereafter?
The boys are ready now

I have a dream
That in the sepia stone streets
Of Jerusalem
Young Palestinian men
And Jewish boys
Will come to grin at the silliness of possession
And give freely to each other
Of their cocks and their assholes—
There's only one temple
It's always been so

The body of a friend

SEX AND DEATH

"I have done with Moby Dick *something that I used to do with my teddy bear, many years ago. I have slept with this piece of perfection in my arms."*

A satisfied customer of Easton Press (from a brochure)

Me too, Easton Press, me too

I never told my mother what happened to my teddy bear
why I threw it away
She said it had sentimental value
I just didn't want to explain it had calcified inside
its stuffing like bone
hard and brittle as toffee

I'd bored a hole up its back when I was 13
pumped on it
with my newfound toy
that hung off my body
My new candy
that got hard as toffee

I fucked that teddy bear
every way imaginable late at night
till, like I said,
it was just bones
hard and brittle inside
from dried semen

I threw it out
and Mom called me ungrateful
I missed the teddy bear sometimes
but I knew it would be highly suspicious to purchase a new
    one at 14
so I tried to read at night to keep my mind off Teddy

I was reading *Moby Dick* for school
the powerful leviathan rising up from underneath
tearing holes in whaling ships
Captain Ahab's leg of bone
the men running their hands through spermaceti

I couldn't go to sea on a whaler myself
but I was hard-bent on *Moby Dick*

I got myself a real nice copy
from the Easton Press

I'd find the pages where the big white whale
sunk a whaler
to gob on the vaseline
Then I'd fuck all through the words
till they spoke stiff as tombstones
sealed the book closed tight as a coffin
calcified a classic
buried its bones in the backyard

Call me Ishmael if you want
Call me Teddy
Like death, I just take what's given
And what's given is a hard and wanting thing
that takes me to the boneyard every time
where I build my temples of stone

IOWA

In Iowa
the corn stiffens and thickens like great virile cocks
above the deep muddy rivers
lolling like teenage boys walking home from school

In Iowa the smokestacks   and the swollen silos
were ready to get on with it
The whistling trains were as unstoppable,
as iron-hard and determined
as that secret something that called me to get naked with a
   man

In Iowa
I tried to run away
but they were everywhere:
The scarecrows with broom handles running through their
   guts
My male classmates who unknowingly and erotically,
   and so carelessly   tortured me
with their veined forearms, lithe shins, and protruding
   adam's apples
Oh the dick is everywhere in the man

In Iowa
even way out in the fields   where I cried
the grasshoppers,
scattered everywhere
like a million penises   poised —
and all of them ready
to jump
again   and again

In Iowa
hot and steamy, sweaty and feverish —
it was an enormous locker room of no escape —
the air was like skin
and the earth and all its plants   like hair
And at night the trains and cats would screech
— and grip

In Iowa
one day
the twister came

And all the earth rose up to meet it
And it was full of all the boys I ever knew —
their forearms and shins, adam's apples and scrotums —
howling with the spiraling phalluses of catlove
swirling with silos and corncobs, scarecrows, smokestacks
  and locomotives
I breathed deep
The breath of god
And I let the entire continent fuck me hard
sucked it right up my asshole
cryin': *Auntie Em, Auntie Em*

It's a good day to get fucked up the ass!

SALAD BOY

I called him Caesar
cuz he was a whole damn salad to me
His fist up my ass like a head of lettuce

When I fucked him
his cock got all red and exploded
like a firecracker in a tomato

His belly was hard and striped as a watermelon
His ass, like 2 ripe mangoes
I wanted to split with a meat cleaver
I did it with a banana instead

The hair in his armpits was like that Japanese seaweed
all dark and funky
His nipples were little cherry tomatoes
I'd suck on until his seeds squirted out

His legs were long and tough as carrots
But his face —
a grizzled beard like croutons
His skin as creamy white as blue cheese dressing underneath
His empty, lost orgasming eyes
Blank as tofu
and his mouth a bitter olive
from which I swallow the pit

OUR LADY OF FRESH PRODUCE

At the organic grocery where he works
they call him Ken
They oughtta call him Keen
for how I wail in this unrequited love

He's dark and gangly S-shaped
He's obscene calligraphy
He's as filthy as the bundles
of certified California organic spinach
that laugh at me from the shelves

He's got the earth coming out of his sallow cheekbones
His eyes swing like spades around the room
which is all soil
—and I'm a weed
I wait for him

He moves like
a cobra
in a melon patch
I can feel his venom
from 30 feet

He came from Oregon
where the faerie holyland is
He's got maple arms
and dark oak legs
He's drenched in sexrain

I wilt like broad-leafed edible greens
Is it the rain?
Or the heat?
Or both?
He's a rainbow either way

Harvest me earth-tearing sower
there's vegetable shrapnel at your feet
and questions about you grow into my ground like carrots
I'll be your pesticide-free crop
your market
and your moon

I write my name
on the back of the mountain
for you

THE BOY FROM PIEDAD

For Gerardo

I lost track of him
Who knows where he's gone
I'm hounded by a corny mysticism
as I travel through Mexico
obsessed with him
Stone faces with his eyes
His cock, a feathered serpent
His asshole like the calendar of the sun
Everything he said
began big
and tapered up into clouds
ending in abstractions
or holiness
A speech of temples

In the broken down streets
of Mexico City
far from the zocalo
a little Indian boy runs across
the street
stops, staring
then reaches out and touches me
before running back

The little boy wasn't you, Gerardo
The only thing in Mexico that wasn't
Or perhaps I've got that backwards

The heart's so inconsistent

And so I watch myself run away
and I think for a second to call out
— *Come back!*
but I don't know the language

JONAS' FIAT

Jonas used to pick me up
and take me to school
in his little yellow Fiat

He was my Spanish teacher

Jonas and I started fucking halfway through the second week
but we never spent the night together
Jonas lived with his family
and I lived with somebody else's

Jonas would take me for long rides
through the mountains
up to Dolores Hidalgo and Guanajuato
Once he fucked me on the hood of the car
I fucked him on the roof
and we screwed endlessly inside

When I got robbed in Mexico City 3 months later
I called Jonas and told him
—all my money, my plane ticket, passport, everything
Jonas said I could drive his car home if I promised to come
   back for good

Jonas and his Fiat, both so sweet

But I'd forgotten about Jonas by the time I got back to San
   Francisco
At night out in the Sonora Desert, I'd pull off to sleep
First I thought about Jonas and jacked off inside
Subsequent nights I moved to the front hood
By the end of the week, as I approached the border,
I was opening the hood and dumping my semen into the
   crankcase
I liked to pull over and piss on the engine when it got hot

When I finally got Jonas' Fiat into my garage at home
it was all I could do not to peel the paint right off its body
I opened all its doors, trunk, hood, windows
I unclamped a fat rubber hose from the radiator
packed it with solvent and fucked Jonas' Fiat
while I revved the carburetor to 4000 rpms with my hand

I wanted to make Jonas' Fiat blow a rod
suck a valve
I wished then I had a metal cock
Ah, but what a poor lover I was for Jonas' Fiat
All I could fuck were his hoses
And no matter how much rubber I wrapped around his
    exhaust pipe
He was just too big and hard for me

But Jonas' Fiat didn't seem to mind
He was some kind of bottom
Long as I gave him gas and oil
He made more noise than any lover I'd ever had
I looked ridiculous at the self-serve station
pumping the hose into Jonas' Fiat with a big hard-on pushing
    out of my pants

I started leaving the oil cap off while I fucked Jonas' Fiat
I liked to watch him pump out his crude, uncontained:
Hot black gushers of 20-weight-50 slopped out of the head of
    the engine
scalded my skin
and ran down my legs

Jonas' Fiat never ran out of cum
I kept a case of it at my feet
and I'd just refill him when he ran low

I still haven't figured out a way to kiss Jonas' Fiat
or get him to stay warm when we sleep
He's awful quiet sometimes
and I sense we both feel kinda bad about Jonas

But in the meantime, I like it rough
I always wanted someone with a cast-iron engine block for a
    body
who could cum so hot he'd brand my flesh with his gism
I think tomorrow I'll have him back up over me and break all
    my ribs
I want to see the guileless look on his face then —
those big round innocent headlights
that say take me home

And maybe then I will

WE STARTED OUT JANITORS

and ended up fuckbuddies
He used to mop the floors without a word
while I vacuumed couches and dusted tables

I figured he didn't speak English
We both figured the other was straight
We started out janitors
Now I clean his asshole with my tongue

It was a restaurant
We both started stealing food from the fridge:
big sausages and blocks of cheese
We started laughing one day when a cube of butter dropped
   out of his pants
as we were locking up to leave
We laughed so fucking hard
and then he said, "I hate this job —
let's take everything and not come back tomorrow"
We started out janitors
Now we're thieves

He said his boyfriend liked pastries as he bagged 3 dozen
   blintzes
I said *I'm queer too*
He said the only thing he liked more than food was sex
I said *You wanna fuck?*
He turned and forced his tongue in my mouth hard
We tore at each other's clothes
We both had big ugly dicks
that we treated like food

We started out janitors
And now we were sucking cock on the kitchen floor
He fucked me as I held the back of a chair
and I came onto his mopped floor
We laughed some more and took all the food

We both showed up the next day
I guess to find each other
Took everything and came back
They didn't fire us
They didn't even notice
We stayed working there for 2 more months

fucking like crazy and cleaning less and less
We started out janitors
Now we're fucking-connoisseurs in a high-class restaurant

We both got fired in the end
for doing a lousy job
— but what did they know
We were investors

We started out janitors
Now we're unemployed fuckbuddies with something better
    to do

DENNY

Denny picked me up
Denny did me
Denny's got a tattoo of his own dick on his belly

Denny's dramatic
Denny's dark
he's nothing like the restaurant I associate with his name
except for maybe the coffee

Denny's got another tattoo
H I V + on his back
in big 6-inch block letters
He says: "I want them to see what they've done"
He's just like Jackie O that way
Denny's demanding
And Denny's never been to Dallas

Denny's reading the *Decameron*
Boccaccio's stories about the plague
Denny's dying of it
Denny don't like it
And Denny don't dance no more

Denny used to do porn
Denny's gotta tattoo of his own dick on his belly
Denny ruined his career with that dick
Denny says it don't matter
He did it, did it, did it on purpose
Denny needed a way out
And he knew 2 dicks ain't better than one

Denny's gotta tattoo of a heart with his own name in it on his
    forearm
Denny's kind of New Age
but Denny's not too smart
Denny's into loving himself   but
Denny doesn't really get it

Denny said he wanted to tattoo my asshole on his chin
Denny could be very funny
Denny was dead serious

Denny got pneumocystis
and Denny gotta new tattoo
Denny gotta skull and crossbones on his forehead
Denny could be very funny
Denny was dead serious
He says: "I want them to see what they've done"
He's just like Jackie O that way
Denny's demanding
And Denny ain't never gonna see Dallas
cuz Denny don't dance no more

BUSBOY SUTRA

Everything about him is long
The Indian nose
The long sling of his chin
cradling the infant soul
He's got spider legs
and monkey arms
and something constant
and stable as stone
in his eyes
of long ago
brown

Long are his lips
twin bridges
cataracts of teeth
The living river inside him
I'm all wet with it

To be with him
would be to be in mountains
a long way away
To travel the river
bending and turning
back
through the steeping stones
where everything changes
to waterfalls
and great swaths
of dizzying flashing brightness
of snow
to the precipitation of him:
Great tears,
beyond emotional correlations
a rain of sparks
from those same eyes
Are they brown and stone
of planets?
Is he the whole universe after all?
I am inside him then
forever
and he in me
Some young man
I've never touched

but seen
and seen beyond
and long back behind
all these pictures
kaleidoscoping this coffee,
this red brick shop, these cars, sycamore trees, voices,
suns and moons in infinitude, mirrors facing mirrors and the
   long roads born of them

And so to sleep naked in his arms
would be as if to gather all the light of the sun
spread all over and bouncing about
It would be to record the memories
of all the stars
That's how improbable
the consummation of this love
How comic
when I've found —
traveling as I've done
the towering pine-treed forests within him
the length of their shadows
echoing his eyelashes
and the ever-changing horizon
mimicked by his mouth —
that we are one inside the other
forever
and inseparable
as the brown is within his eyes
as water and stone

The universe is love made
and making
So why do I lust for him
as if we don't share that already?

There is no need for introductions then
I set him free
for we are in love regardless
of what we may either believe
and all my longing draws
a big circle
like a comet orbiting

I'd love to see him again sometime too
in a hundred years, or a million
—or tomorrow even

For now,
I sing—
for him and for me
and for all who see what I see
—this song

BIRDS

He watches me and I watch him

The boy at the Grillburger
Is like a crow
Shoulders slightly hunched
Around his broad chest
That I spy at the neckline of his bright white t-shirt
Is pale Indian
In contrast to the deep brown of his face, framed in black chin
   whiskers
And dark eyes below the shadow of his buzz cut

It's the same with his forearms (and I'm sure the small of his
   back)
Fading from brown to milky cappuccino as his biceps swell
Strongest and most tender part of him

I speak of his plumage

But it's the watching above all else
The face of an owl
His eyes so wide
Is it wisdom then that draws me to his body?

Old sailor that I am (all homosexuals are old sailors of desire,
   in time)
I've got him doing acrobatics back in the kitchen
But no matter how I twist him about
I am arrested by those eyes
Startled
Watching

Bird of prey
And I thought I had to capture *him*
Either way is fine by me
The glove of a falconer
Or his talons in my neck

Hunter and hunted
Prey and predator
White boy and brown boy
Soft and hard
Him and me

Life and death

This sweet gift of heaven:
Homosexuality
That merges all differences
In the grappling of desire
The spilling of seed
And the resting together
as one boy
The universal boy
The godboy
We are blest
We share that

Till the wings move again
Flutter, flap
And we return to the old world
Of misunderstanding
And separateness
Birds on a single wire

He watches me and I watch him

TEA in the TENDERLOIN

Miz Brown's Feedbag was hardly a romantic setting
But broken boys have anniversaries where they can
And right now, I couldn't think of a better way to celebrate
  him
These whipped mashed potatoes, as white and gravy-
  smothered as his ass
Crowned by a cube of yellow butter, hot and running like my
  cum shot on the whole mess

I let my milk spill and run down my chin as I smile at him
  and lick it off my stubble
He's having chicken
—they say that's what humans taste like

We've got a couple wishbones to share for later
I wonder if maybe his green peas are the beads of that rosary
I shoved up his ass 2 nights ago
My meatballs are dark and musty like his armpits
I roll them on my tongue like his hairy balls

"Let's get the fuck out of here and go get a beer," he
  impetuously remarks,
tossing a crumpled ten dollar bill on the counter like an old
  cum rag
I agree, thinking I'd love to go drink his piss

HUSTLER

He had a bank card for a cock
He'd insert it into horny old men with money
He knew all the right buttons to push
and he'd thrust his beautiful credit
in over and over again
pumpin' his payback
while the machine groaned
and made those chirping sounds
like a bird
$20 for every thrust
Bang, Bang, Bang
And the twenties would pop out like blackheads
Bang, Bang, Bang
Like a slot machine
He was a one-organed bandit
and he laughed when he saw the oranges
and the apples
line up in rows in the old man's eyes

MY TYPE

He's the only hot man alive
in a city of a million faggots
He's doin' the David Koresh thing to me
and I believe in *one* god
just one
cuz he
He's my type

He's my stigmata
He's my 2X4s fashioned into a crucifix
He's my 9-inch nails
He's my type

He makes my heart do the sunflower thing
following him like he's the sun crossing my days
See,   he's a star
And he ain't no red dwarf either
He ain't no supernova
He's just a yellow star
the kind that sustains life
    my kind
        my type

He's like my dick
after too much sex
He won't do what I want him to do
He won't be what I want him to be
He's as frustrating as growing old
cuz he's my type

He's a drunk walking around with a loaded pistol
doing target practice on my heart
and even when he ain't
I'm his dog
I chase his stray bullets and bring them back to him
to shoot again
Hey   he don't mind
and neither do I
He's my type

He held me like my mother once
He communicates like my dad
He's as sexy and mean as my brother

He's my evil twin
separated at birth
And yeah
He's my type

He touches me when he sees me
gets all excited and warm
Every hug is like an enormous apology for bein' a flake
He likes me so much
He says he thinks about me all the time
Then he gets stoned and forgets
He never calls
He's fulla "whoops"es and "slipped my mind"s
He treats me kinda bad
See, he's fulla "I think so"s and "maybe I'll see ya there"s in a
   city of "just not sure"s
He's full of shit
And when all is said and done
He's   just   my type

He draws beautiful pictures
and writes pretty good poems
He's all fucked up
but there's something wonderful in his spirit
he don't like no one to see
I wanna fuck it—and sometimes I do
His body's a jungle though
that I hack away at with the machete of "tell me your story
   come on tell me your story"
But it never ends
and he never tells
cuz he's my type

I wish he weren't afraid of me
He's sure he isn't
But he's running away
I'd never hurt him
He hates the power he says I give him
and he likes rough sex
like I gotta literally ratchet his nipples
He wishes I'd really abuse him
but he's so precious
He'll never get what he wants from me
nor I from him

Figures
He's my type

I guess he's playing hard to get
whatever that means
And I doubt he knows he's doing it
I guess I'm a fool
and when I oughta be telling him to *fuck off*
I'm feeling sorry for the poor thing
He's so afraid
He's so maimed
He's got no one in the world
–and he don't want no one either
And he don't want me
He's a broken-hearted child
wounded puppy and all that
He's a confusing, inconsiderate motherfucker
I love him so
And he don't care
I don't know what I am to him
And he ain't tellin'
He's a blessed mess who don't know which way he's going
He's fulla "see ya soon"s and "call ya later"s
He's my favorite broken toy
He'll never hear this poem
and if he does –
He won't answer, he won't hear
He's fragile as glass
the tough little punk
He's...
ya know...   my type

JUST DO IT

Horseshit on his shoes
His jeans smell like wet dog
So strip the sexy bastard—
belt, pants down, his hairy legs kicking to help
The shrapnel scar on his knee breaks my heart
but his is closed for business
So I stand on the streetcorner of our love
like one of those guys shaking a cardboard sign

This is how I spend my longing
tearing off his clothes
He watches me with a hint of suspicion
a passive *fuck you* on his brow
There's lint in his bellybutton
his pubic hair pressed flat
cuz he doesn't shower often
His cock blue-gray-brown Mexican
hard and curved
His balls big and loose
His ass like a stallion's
I don't know why I want his cum so bad
He's a lousy kisser
And fucking him feels like crying

PARIS, TEXAS

Big sundown
purple
Houston highrise
buttes
your thoughts
stand like sentinels
in the desert

Lovely Gregory
watchful brightness
spring flower of the wasteland
flash flood in the desert
fragile as morning
close as the heat
angry as the sun
forlorn as this dry earth

Your heart
sonic boom in empty places
roars with laughter
shows its teeth
flashing
makes all the trailerhomes rattle in the heat

My memory   is
strung like a wire across the Great Basin
You're hanging all over it like laundry
flapping in the wind
your eyes and mouth flashing like glare
settling like a mirage

I had a head-on collision with you
in the emptiness of desert roadway
and I laugh
from my hospital bed
Metal-bending blessing
You are rain wrecking sandstone

Parched bones
and buzzing sounds
desert butte flood
flower blessing
mineral magnificent

laughter
like water
If I tried not to love you
I couldn't love the earth
which ain't possible

This desert lives
by tears alone
blessed one
by tears alone

BUBBLE

He's made of small tight circles
each bordered all around by long black lashes
Tattoos run up his arms
and I surmise
other limbs and stretches of his bark-dark skin
They are stories and tales that climb like moss along tree
    branches
in Northwestern rainy forests
Or they're like those maps left behind by mystical termites
exposed when bark sheds fallen pine trees
in the mountains beyond Yosemite
What secret route do they tell?
Where do they go?
What promised land sought the termites?
And are they there now?
And how could it be more wonderful than Yosemite?
Is it possible do you think?

All questions are consumed in the fire of wonder
And his hair
is free and roiling, boiling
as smoke
There's nothing he can do about it,
the 4-year-old-boy madness of its play
His waist rides low
like a Harley chopper
for he's stalky
Tight, small circles
river rocks
and water eddying
way down in valleys
where meadows lie
and flowers bloom
popping and pirouetting in the wind

He's like the many moons of Jupiter
and bubbles that burst
about the heads of children
It's a powerful little body that he carries
like a tight little fistful of gumballs
The envy of other little boys nearby
—among them me!
We all long to fill our mouths with the multicolored

kid-like chaotic marbles of chewing,
precious and highly prized
for the slippery sweetness
they'll set free upon our tongue

His little booted feet
have kicked me
His knobby knees elbow my sides
that split with laughter
as I roll onto the floor
A little sowbug
in sweetest danger

He's the boy rolling fast
a giant tire down a road
bounding with rubbery glee

We're 2 balls bouncing
loosed from the playground
by wild kicking children
and ricocheting
through traffic
and parking meters
and over the heads of pedestrians
through tunnels
and precariously over suspension bridges
Up over hedges
and down harrowing alleyways
past red and yellowbright signs
that with frustration
seek to guide us on our laughing, sprung path

That big yellow ball
that falls down finally each day
—and the moon that rolls on through behind it
lay us low in time
We come upon an empty field
our bouncing and our ricocheting spent
and finally winding to a sputter
long to rest the one against the other

And after the cool giggling evening of crickets
and all things that jump and sing:
What must it be like to lie as river stones with him
under a thousand stars

that make the water
shimmer above us
like his smile?

MY IRA BOY

I wouldn't go on hunger strike for my country
but I'd agree to live solely off your semen
for so little as your Irish eyes smiling
I'd give up other men
and my U.S. citizenship
for the prison of your crotch
I'd swallow your holy roman seed
like the host

Imagine if there were another Reformation
— this time of male beauty —
I'd stay a papist too
And if they split me like your nation—
(but only you can split me, my republican brother)
— Oh, I'm just not political enough to join the IRA
But I'd cheer on the rioting of your cock
in the Belfast streets of my ass
I'd smile to see your cock raised like the Irish flag
and firing like a salute at those IRA funerals
Oh, if my mouth could be all those pubs you've bombed
If my ass could be the London Subway

Our passion is too pure for English negotiation
and I like too much the wild gun-running sweat on your chest
the taste of sulfur in your kiss
and the dynamite hidden away in the luscious peetbog of
   your ass

I'm a patriot of your body
and that alone
I'll not starve for anything
I'll live solely off your cock
A good catholic never rejects the host they say
and you are my shepherd
boy
You have all my faith

So I'll not go on hunger strike
but I'll boycott protestant semen if it'll make you happy
Just lock me up for life
in your arms

'til our nation
(you and me)

           is one

FRATERNITY

They told me it was about brotherhood
but mostly it was a dubious dabbling in drunk-driving
  delirium
doped up and holed up behind a great cement dam
entombed in the nursery of the straight white male hydro-
  electric powerplant
where Daddy turned all the levers

These were the princes of the powerbrokers
drunk, dumb, and dosed
in the dungeons of consciousness
And I was running from queer demons
hiding behind walls as thick as these
—they had to be safe

I hid among the big whirring dynamos of electrical boysex
generating the glowing germs of desire
like fireflies I couldn't not see
I ran in place for 4 years
impressed by turbines and flumes

Drunken I debated delicious dick dichotomy
trying to convince myself it was envy for their sex not greed
  for it
I lost every case
and was sentenced by my penis to hard labor
in a fraternity
I was in a prison made of my own passion
The bars of my cell
were big hard blue-veined cocks
I shook them and I wailed
for release

My dreams were kinder to me though
flowering like the blossoms of ripe phalli
floating like lotus flowers on a warm white sea of fresh
  boycum
flowing from the frightened eyes of these sexy scared boys
  even
who cried subconsciously for me
—I know they did
They cried for me and they cried for themselves

We cried in brotherhood without ever letting on
for the boy in us all
who was killed when the bell of initiation into this frat
   manhood thing rang
That was the only brotherhood we really ever had
A brotherhood of loss
like our dicks setting down like the sun
when they could have drove deep and found a place to swim
   upstream
Upstream where the river still ran wild
and none of them ever knew
that I sauntered in a solitary
subversion of semen somnambulance
because I was a fag

I'd say it was a heaven
but delicious dick dichotomy determined
it was purgatory
They had these things called "Brotherhoods"
in which they dominated the new pledges
The older boys made us strip and do calisthenics
We were so close
to just letting it go
The room was full of sweat and groaning
so close to realizing my fantasies
and maybe a few others'
We would have done anything the older boys said
to achieve brotherhood

We would have paired up and fucked each other all night
for brotherhood
We would have gotten on our knees for the older guys we so
   wanted approval from
for brotherhood
We would have let them fuck us and welcome us home
We would have sucked each other's 18-year-old stems
For brotherhood

For brotherhood
we would have cummed for distance
instead of vomiting for distance
Ain't it the same thing sublimated?
I mean 4 years of watching these guys guzzle beer
It always seemed like they were trying to prove to one
   another

what great cocksuckers
they could have been
How much they could take
like randy Marlon Brandos on the waterfront:
"I coulda been a cocksucker.
You shoulda watched out for me, Charlie
—you was my brother."
Brotherhood

And I felt sorry for them
trapped behind that Hoover Dam
that made them strive for 52 years
Their Daddy's age, stamped on the fuselage of a B-52 bomber
the age of power and privilege
not a place for boys or cocksuckers
Their steel-vault hearts I see even today on the streets of this
   city
10 years later
They could have broken like eggs full of semen
They could have been take-off-that-tie sloppy and sticky
in boy-romping randiness
They didn't have to be fags forever
For brotherhood

But youth wasn't worth much
to these beautiful adonises
Women didn't want it
and their father's laughed at it
considered it a liability
Like a flower was somehow just something trivial preceding a
   fruit

They couldn't bear their mothers' love
how she thought they were cute
It compromised them into powerless obscurity
So they pretended to prefer the patriarchy's practicality about
   produce
I think that fags and mothers were the only ones who loved
   them for what they were:
Beautiful little boys unbeknownst
bearing their beautified boners
like bamboo and bougainvillea

Power was all they were provided as a goal
so pansies and petunias be damned

They played their volleyball games
They got their grades and connections for grad school
They harvested their friendships and their fathers
They got their muscles all hard and tight
sleek as machinery
—not for the girls,
but for the other boys

For power over other boys
For intimidation
For a kind of hierarchy
My dick is bigger than yours kind of thing
I got more horses of power under my hood
A certain kind of brotherhood
And that's all a big dick was
a pecking pecker order
For brotherhood
–as in older brother and younger brother

For true brotherhood
the things I could have shown them
The fields of wildflowers non-fruit-bearing I could have led
   them through
We were all the same age,
generally the same size and strength
A big dick and a smaller one are not that different
in the grand scheme of things now, are they?
Not among brothers
In the grand scheme of things
like stars and liberty
equality and fraternity
For brotherhood carries no judgment
Brotherhood does mean love, you know
A kind they were afraid of

And yet it was what this living arrangement was supposed to
   be about
Was it a fascination then with something that they couldn't
   have
that made them talk about it and claim they had it?
Like how the African American girls straightened their hair,
the sissies lifted weights to look like football stars
And me—
I joined a fraternity to be a straight boy
and convince myself everything would be okay

and I will find protection
from losing the love of my family and friends
and so many strangers
without which, I shall die

Were they trying to prove that they could actually be a team?
Yet, competition was the priority always
And if the team didn't serve that—
well, no one gets rich at a co-op
Their teams were more like alliances I guess
NATO and all that, a common enemy
But real brotherhood—it bankrupted enmity

Their brotherhood was relegated to language alone
They were trained to fight, fight, fight
Even for brotherhood they were told
Alone, afraid, loading rifles of manproof
Oh, I would say again we had a brotherhood in this way
I was there too protecting my fragile manhood slipping away
They never knew
my sexual subversions
They too walked in a solitary semen somnambulance
their life asleep in their testicles

Was it a fascination with something that they couldn't have?
The whole man-frat thing sure was for me
It was the central theme of my queer childhood
Before I knew what these feelings were,
there were feelings of longing to be another little boy
I wanted to be the beautiful blond baseball-playing boy
until my hairless little cock
stood straight up and pointed at him
"That one there; that's who you want to be"
I remember crying for a long time in my bed one night
when I was only 7
when I accepted that I would give up my family, my room, all
    my toys and all my friends—and Jesus too—
to be that boy
I had 3 brothers who hated my guts
They would've loved that little blond boy
I couldn't be

No wonder it was sadness I saw
when I first looked upon my male seed in my hand
I'd missed my mark

Oh, if my penis had been a boy-seeking missile
or a bird of prey boy-bound

So the frat was a twisted sort of blessing
like a nest I'd stumbled into
And all that longing came back
A dormant seed watered by alcohol in drunken reveries
A nest of beautiful bacchanalian boyness
A cock nest

And they were working like bees
honeycombing the college
with hexagonal cum compartments as they masturbated in
   bathroom stalls
and the private cubicles of the library
I wished then my asshole was 6-sided
Oh Cinderella lonely queer I'd long
If the cock fits, wear it!

I dreamed one might be my prince
but I knew   I knew
We all were princes and we all fit each other perfectly
For brotherhood I longed
The brotherhood they'd each accepted initiation into
And I couldn't just offer up my toys and Jesus and family
   anymore
My hairless little dick
was a loaded .357 Magnum now
and my desires felt dangerous

They told me the frat would make me a man
And I thought   *Good!*
Cuz I'm slippin' into womanhood real fast!
            Oh, when does a boy become a man?
When he signs a contract of brotherhood he plans to break?
When he stops caring that words have meaning?
When he accepts *I'm a Zete* as a tag of brotherhood
simply because it has status and the love be damned?
When he decides once and for all to bow down to Daddy
and suck the dick of his dogma instead of the dick of his
   friend?

It was happening before my eyes too soon
They were teen-something, twenty-something young guys
When does a boy become a man?

As soon as his cock drops I'd say
dropping into manhood
every one of 'em
like virile bombs out of the lumbering B-52s that were their
    fathers
because they couldn't find brotherhood
No one had shown them a way
And I could have but was afraid

And crossing the river Styx was the first trial most would
    have turned from
Our sticks straining together forcing the pussywillow off the bough
and into a fabulous fellatiated flower full of pollen
For brotherhood I longed
I even *lied*   with them
For Brotherhood
—Oh so close
To lie with them is only a conjugation away

But like the rules of language
the rules of the fathers kept our dicks apart
But still, for brotherhood I longed
It's what they promised me, you know
I who would never fit in
I who knew how to be a brother to them
I was the only one who knew

I was silent
And so they told me over and over again
—because I was a lie of what they were and that made them
    trust me—
how well I fit in
And all I could imagine
as I watched their lips pronounce it:
fit
How would I fit in each of them?
In their assholes, in their mouths
How well all of them could fit and fill me
fit and fill each other
Oh brothers
I dreamed of wild fucking orgies
And I no longer believe they were an impossibility
We all wanted brotherhood
For brotherhood
I think we all could've given ourselves to one epiphany

But my dreams went limp and I left
        left with no memory of union
— only an infinite repertoire of masturbation material
The steamy showers
and their half-hard boycocks risen from sleep
The tender lines of hair that vertically descended between
    their bellies and their belts
like Chinese writing
I was cheated of the same thing they were
so I'm not bitter
We wanted brotherhood
and none of us got it

And I see it in their eyes today
receded far inward beyond their gray suits
that have formlessly canceled their male beauty
behind a wall of shapeless fabric
that only speaks for the power of the man
not the boy-joy springloaded flowery semen stem
which I hope   *I do hope*
their wives can retrieve something of
as they race into middle age after the spoils
the kingmakers promised

I hug them now when I see them on the businessman's
    boydead streets
It's a sort of brotherhood I think
that they can still let themselves touch
I hated them for years for refusing to touch me
until I thought of brotherhood and what it could be
And maybe I am the only one of us who knows
        I better get to work teaching then

So now I feel a sad lost love for these boys
For what we intended together
Even if we failed
We were all scared, brainwashed and running
lost in the deafening deluge of the whirring dynamos of
    electrical boysex
generating the glowing germs of desire
that made us blind and vulnerable to the dogma of B-52s
And how much like 52 they are today

But I know what hangs between their legs is always young
A penis is forever a boy

And when it rises like the sun
it gives the boy in the man away

So these so-called men
are always boys to me
I hug them close
I lean forward into their arms
and wish them well
I give them my gift of brotherhood longed for
—Otherwise I'll long forever
And besides, I know it's what they want
For brotherhood is how we met
and what we dreamed upon together
10 long years ago

For Brotherhood
I would have mounted them and left them my seed
the gift of spring
like a lucky bag of Indian corn
they could carry through the valley of death
of being a straight white male businessman

And I could have used their lucky bag in those hard years too
Oh, and even if it's only the scrap metal
of a plane that crashed in a field of wildflowers,
there is a kind of brotherhood still salvageable in their eyes
I lean forward and hold them
I wish them well as brothers

And at night in my dreams I fall backward into their arms
Into the arms of 40 naked athletic boys alive
and scented with sweat
sitting on the young fine fence of 20 years give or take
I'll give
And bless the boyhood that still breathes in them

THE BOY with the POUTING LIP

Is it heavy I wonder?
Does it tire his jaw?
It's not dullness that makes that fat lower lip of his pout
A too-big petal perhaps
on the flower of youth

He's nothing special on some level
Who is?
Such is age that we lose that old romantic view
of the messianic young man
He'll save nothing—
perhaps a little money in time
The best ones save some talisman of young boy love
—a gesture, a twinkle, a grin, some corner of their heart
  unsullied

What then becomes of such a lip?
I've loved 2 or 3 with such a mouth
My heart hangs heavy and plump at the thought
—Oh no, it's not dullness!
It'll likely drag down his jowls over the years
obliterate whatever angles there are in his chin
He'll die like a fish
his mouth gaping

May he be caught far upstream then
having returned…
May he die in that beautiful place
under the big pines
and the massive granite,
the quiet
and the flower petals
that acknowledge his perfection
and this poem
of which he never knew
nor read

SHOOTING STAR

He came like any other
In a corner sipping tea
Eyeing me
"How you doin'?" I chanced
"Okay, dude," and he kicked the chair leg opposite him
An invitation to sit

We spoke of the rain
Which led to his truck and his horses
Mostly I was fascinated by his naïveté
"I got no gaydar, dude"
He was just back from Iraq
"I was there twice"
And the shrapnel scar he shows me on his knee

"I wasn't afraid," he said defiantly
Nor am I, I think to myself
As he told me how he came home to therapy and Zoloft
The foster homes as a child
"My parents never wanted me; I was a mistake.
I joined up because *what else was I gonna do?*"

"What's the worse thing you saw?" I asked
"Charred bodies — you could still see their penises, just burnt
  black things.
-Oh, and the women and children ground into the pavement
  like roadkill. You know, like black stains?"
And he said it without feeling
"Did you ever shoot anybody?"
"No, we just ran over people already shot a long time ago;
I was a radio man
I think it's the wrong war
But I'm Marine Corps"

I nodded.

He brings that up later as we move into sex
"I'm a top," he says, "this'll never work."
"I'm not about that," I tell him
I lick the shrapnel scar on his knee
"I don't know," he muses, "I can't imagine it. It's kinda like
  what the Marines say:
I came to conquer, not to bow."

I think it sounds stupid, as stupid as war
But I will not judge him
I am a Buddhist
I came to bow not to conquer

He calls all the time for a while
Then he disappears
I am not so young to be a fool for love
I bow
I whisper
His name
Again and again

Then out of the blue: *He's been busy, how about next week?*
All day, lying about
I give him a tarot reading with no great news
He wants to learn, and so he fakes a reading for me
All about this new young man I've met
and how important it is for me to know him and become his
    friend

After all his talk of never being afraid, I come to pity him
He'll make me cry, I think to myself
Again and again
You'll be lucky the day he goes
He looks at me now in a way that makes me think he'll never
    leave
But also that he can't afford to look at anyone like that again
    or often

I'd do foolish things for him
Against my better judgment
His parents didn't want him
But the Marine Corps did
Shock and Awe
Tracers in the nightsky

Those who care and those who don't

He vanished next time for good

Shooting star
Warrior

No honor among thieves
But the light's the same

Only brighter

SOLDIERS

The boys in the glass case at the library are hot
The girls know it
The boys like me know it
The kids know it
Even the old men and women know it
Though for them it's the heat of stove and radiator
A comfort
For them, the boys in the glass case are money in the bank

For the children, the boys in the glass case, in their uniforms,
    are superheroes
Their stern willful eyes intent to do what's right
To the girls, these bulletproof glass boys are a man to guard
    the house
A man worthy to woo their maidenhead
But to boys like me, these fragile glass boys are raw and
    packed as tightly as explosives
No safer in my army than the enemy's
They are a conundrum
Shards that cut and shimmer in the light
A weapon
And I want their war, like we all want their war
But not a killing war, an offensive or a defensive war, not a
    war aimed outward at all
I alone, and those like me, care about who they encounter
I alone, the invert
desire their enemy as much as I desire them
desire not their return with a belt of scalps
But the grin of a contest won
A competition resolved, bloodless, but the ground wet all the
    same
With sweat and semen, saliva
The boys in the glass case are an aquarium of beautiful,
    poison fish

The boys in the glass case at the library are hot as electric eels
It's only the boys their age won't say so
To themselves or others
The boys their age are either less stupid, less driven, less
    egotistical, less fucked-up
Or less patriotic (which doesn't mean what people think)
Patriotism is as blind as Pilate's justice
And Jesus did it for us

Real men who love Jesus don't have to die, the other boys tell
    themselves
The boys in the glass case challenge them all the same
Threaten them with a blunt weapon of manhood
Far clearer than the convoluted abstract power of these other
    boys' blades of knowledge and money
Jesus, sure, but for a boy to be a man he has to do it himself, the
    boys in the case answer

The boys in the glass case at the library are hot
And sometimes they change
Like weather
Some are removed
Others spawn displays of dozens more photos
A storm of reminisce
These are the dead, preserved in amber
Those whose photos disappear
have served and returned home
To be forgotten with their scars
The dead are the real stars here
At the library, in the glass case
On display
Their sacrifice dressed up in celebrity and religion
To drown out their last whimper
Their doubt
Even their courage
Which every dying man knows is a humble thing
He would not want to see enshrined

The boys in the glass case at the library are hot
And I didn't want to think so at first
Hector, John, Scott, Jared, Victor, Eduardo, Alonzo, Enrique,
    Tyrone
Their faces transfix me
Like Edward Curtis Indians
Warriors
What then is this glory in war?
I thought war might end in my lifetime
A land of milk and honey, the Middle East
A prosperous Africa too
Religion fading, freeing the Irish, the subcontinent, Sri Lanka,
    Israel,
The homosexuals of Mississippi and Brazil
That we could outgrow violence
I know now we never will

I learned it at the library
So long as sperm churns
There will be aim and there will be invasion
Surrender, gunplay, mayhem, the earth soaked with
Human fluids
They'll keep making up reasons
But it's just the way of men

And the boys in the glass case at the library are hot
As fire
It is their lot
And we are cool and unburned
We do not know them
We flirt with their warmth
The child who can get them to smile and pat their head
The old folks who receive their bow, their submission to the
    common myth
 (A little payback makes them feel warm as brandy)
For the women, the boys encased
Are a promise of mammalian bliss, enveloping them from
    behind
For the other young men, their unscorched rivals:
Bad luck, sucker, bummer, glad it's not me;
One less threat on the street, in a bar, on a field where they
    bang their fragile manhood against one another
To shatter
For all these others, the boys in the glass case are but warriors
    tempered and tamed

But for boys like me
We alone dream the dream of fuel
To be burned clean into Buddhist nothingness
By the boys in the glass case
By the fire of their tongues, their lips, their bristled, scruffed
    chins crackling; the rough fabric of their buzz cuts burning;
    their time-bomb-ticking flacid cocks — the hot iron of their
    erections
 The molten release — saliva, sweat, semen
 The burning of their penetration
 The shock and the awe

 We long for them to melt the glass and spend all their war in
    us

THANKSGIVING

For Squanto

His balls must have been as plump as a bird's breast
Visions of grabbing hold of his drumsticks
And stuffing him full of sweet potatoes

Teeth banging together
Men get too hungry
Their mouths fill with cranberries
Unable to enjoy each other's company
Or even thank each other
Without a little bloodshed
Eh, Squanto?

Pass the cabernet

His gravy oozing all over
the steaming hot mashed potatoes of London lads
shoveled up his ass in dollops

Jam on that yam, man

They'd always thought a nice ass
Was like pie
They got a pie in the face

Because History's a clown

Sodomy wasn't allowed in Christian Europe
Was it, Cromwell?
And then land ho,
Squanto's willing fat uncut cock
His muscular brown ass

Gratefulness

Or too much of a good thing

Squanto had plenty of dick already

And besides, the thing about thank yous
Is that they're almost always cursory
And followed by demands for more

And we all kill the thing we love

THESE ARE THE PLACES WHERE I AM BROKEN

A pay phone in Yosemite Valley
where I called David to tell him
I was going to be a suicide
Because I had come here to the mountains
believing
that stone was my mother
and she had turned her shoulder
and all her rivers tears

These are the places where I am broken
The Psychiatric Clinic
he convinced me to check into
There are scabs on my wrists
"I know, I know" he said
"Just try the medication, if it doesn't work
you have my blessing—do it"

These are the places where I am broken
On a street in Vancouver Canada when I was only 11
where my father pointed out a man walking
and said, "Look at that fag
Look at that fuckin faggot"
And I knew, I knew

These are the places
And my bedroom 3 days later
where I woke up screaming
and my legs wouldn't move
and I told my mother I was a homosexual
and she said no, no   *it's just nerves*
and never remembered afterward my words

My words
My words
These are the places

On Folsom Street
where he told me that I was a pig
a white middle-class pig
And then only 2 weeks later he was gone
And turned up an OD.

at the Denver City Morgue
And I have never even been to Denver
It is a place I have been broken

And I keep seeing the 6-inch scars
running up both his arms
we shared that jewelry
I see his scars in my dreams
running like the dashed line highway
out across the salt flats

I would have gone with him

The kanji tattoo on his neck
like a stamp
by the county coroner
another casualty — didn't make it
finalized
That was my stamp you bastard
That was my heart
my heart
Those were his words

And these are the places
A hospice on Diamond Street
where hundreds of faggots have died
some of them my friends
Diamonds discarded
and not all of them died like Wayne
who went like the sun
and made us all jump like crickets or frogs
so powerful was his resurrection
was his shattering glass ending

These are the places
In a courtroom
when he threw a cup of coffee at me
And he tried to strangle me
in front of the judge
And as they dragged him away
"You haven't seen the last of me"
And the violence and the court orders and arrests that
    followed
in front of the gate of my house

which has become a shack glued together by tears
I had loved this broken vase

These are the places where I am broken
On the school playground
where he bullied and kicked me
calling me a fag
in front of douglas fir
in front of cloud
in front of sky,
in front of sun
And now none of those things can ever come unglued from
    sorrow
from that moment, which is a feeling, of humiliation and loss

These are the places where I am broken
And as I break
everything around me fuses
together
The places where I have broken are the places where I am
    stuck
I am not talking about entropy
I am talking about the consummation of experience and
    sorrow
I am talking about fucking
I am talking about Denver and Vancouver
I am talking about the playground and Folsom Street
I am talking about a hospice and my bedroom
I am talking about a mental hospital
And I am talking about the fact
that if you lived long enough you would meet sorrow
everywhere eventually
and you wouldn't be able to stand it
You'd be like a fly in amber
and you would beg to die
God Bless entropy
I am not talking about entropy
Or the decay of Vince's OD'd body
I am talking about Vince's tattoos
I am talking about his neck and his arms
I am talking about the finality and elegance of his 6-inch scars
These are the places
I am talking about the courtroom
and the wince on Colin's face as the police cuff his wrists
because he does not know how to love

I am talking about millions of eons that made the stone of
   Yosemite
I am talking about reincarnation
and the habits of hell
I am talking about yesterday fucking today
and the deformed baby that is born tomorrow
I'm not talking about entropy
God Bless entropy
I am talking about glue
And as everything falls around me
like rain and mudslide
despair builds an edifice
like a tomb
to keep me contained
to give me a home
I could not find outside
And that tomb is the place I will finally break
These are the places
And if I am Wayne
If I am Wayne
God, nothing matters now but to be Wayne
Then it will be the breaking of the husk of a seed
It will be ground
it will be soil
It will be a final place
This is the final place…
And the breaking will be as bread

THE CASTRO

It was ours
Whoever we were
A sexual minority
A sexual ministry
A people set free
A people comforted
A people hounded and dying
A people endured

Love is small
But sustaining
Like a cumshot
And we produced more of those
Per square inch
Than any people in any place on earth
In all of time
That's how we survived
They'll tell you otherwise
Those who love their chains
They'll say we paid for our freedom
They'll say that sex almost did us in
But sex is what saved us in fact
It's just like love that way

IN PRAISE of GODS
and OTHER HEAVENLY BODIES

MILAREPA

Was a stray cat we found
We thought: "Who knows,
maybe bodhisattvas come back as cats sometimes"

We fed him,
gave him a place to sleep,
and watched for signs

But all he ever did was fuck and fight his way through the
  night
We called it crazy wisdom
and did the same

DICK PRAYER

Oh, the landscape of his penis
The rivers and fissures that run
I wanna row down them all
I want to camp in the forest of his pubic hair
and roll around with his balls
I want to explore the scarred land
of his circumcision
like badlands
like battlefield
like dry parched desert
I wanna lick and bring it rain

His dick is trying to tell me something
like how the land does
without words
but by what comes out of it
and how it smells
By how it changes
by it's texture
It's rockhard
It's full of water
It's bouncing in the air
It's a firestick, a torch
And my asshole is dark
My mouth is dark
His dick brings light to my inner world

It's so beautiful
I want to thank it
and he it hangs off of
And whoever created this thing
This cockscape
which has taught me so much about the land
and made me love the earth so much

The earth is a dick
and you need to let it fuck you
You need to suck it:
Go thou and stroke the trees
enter the waters
Let the wind spread you across the sky
and let its storms explode inside you
Treat the world like a beautiful cock

Have fun with it and honor it as a divine thing
Go thou and worship dick
Do it with all your body and all your heart

RELIGION

There are more cocks than saints
and they are as distinguished by their qualities
Patrons of pumping
martyred as they shoot their wads and cockdie on sexy
washboard stomachs
I like the black-haired ones best
I like the mystery they're coming out of
I like the light that comes out of darkness
White mushrooms and black logs
White mushroom clouds of cum exploding out of black
  missiles
White flowers on black lava
Stars at night
Moon in a black sky
White cum and black men
White teeth, white eyes, white Calvin Kleins
His black cock, his white cum
Black snake, white tongue

CRUISING

All the lonely nights
colorful
all stacked like fruit
—they have to be

And I can
juggle
bowling pins
on fire
in the sky
like jets
fast-looking
into
an endless
horizon
blue-white
and round
breaking the sound
barrier
—talk to me
  like lemons
  squirting
  eyes
  tart
  alive
  and
  dying
  in a cup
  of tea
  conjugal

MAKE MY BOYFRIEND A BUDDHA

I keep thinking about the day you die
And I gotta believe in reincarnation
I can't live with the thought that you'll never be again
Oh the gods will not know what to do with you
As you sure as hell as you never knew what to do with
   yourself
They'll probably make you one of the 10,000 Buddhas
confounded by your beauty and your fury

He's so fucking sexy, they'll conclude
He'll inspire devotion in millions
Let's give him a pure land
Let's give him a deva realm
with his cock dorje
and his scrotum bell
All his joints are mala beads
and his skin like milk and saffron
            Mandalas for eyes
His words are sacred koans
and his ass is one fine lotus seat

Oh   I keep thinking about the day you die

Oh my Buddha boyfriend
I could make an altar to you then
keep you here within my arms
But what relics have you left me?
I've not an ounce of your piss or spit,
your fine smooth cum

And I keep thinking about the day you die
I know that rainbows will arc up across the sky
like how your back used to do
when you'd spurt
and devas will cry out
in your white rain falling lotus-petaled gift

Let Manjushri circumcise me then
I'm lost in the sandy unsure ground of grief
the colored pathways of the palace of the Kalachakra
all leading toward destruction with a big Tibetan laugh

Oh make my boyfriend a Buddha!

FAERIE GATHERING

Wolf Creek is one big 80-acre faggot
I've got a crush on

These 10 days   have been
like one   long   slow   delicious   fuck
looking into that lovely faerie face
I can feel the smooth friction of the muddy land entering me

I see the shadows of his faerie wings
flitting across the moonlight
My body has become a pattern of magick tokens
offerings to this Great Faggot Spirit

My asshole opens like a rising sun to receive his hot Oregon
   day
Each morning   I open my lips   to kiss his faerie
   skymouth
and out rolls a purple moondisc from his smile

Oh my Whitman cock
sings like a cricket in his sweatdrenched night
and paints a Jackson Pollock out of blackberries and limestone

All the daylong I lick his drygrass chest
and hold his treebranch limbs
I watch him piss the clear coolness of the spring

I run through his red earth
like tears and blood and cum and mud and honey
         I like the bees that swarm around him
They're the faeries
Comin' for to carry me home

My chest is an altar
I've erected to my Wolfboy
and my heart dances under his moongaze
My arms move like my tongue through his breath
I whistle the pipes of Pan
rolling like an echo through the woods
I contort my body into a kiss inside his meadowmouth
All these forested hills are his goatee

I squirm around in his warm muddiness
I sing to him with my blood
My orifices echo with his laughter
—they are the pores of his skin

I bathe in his eyes
like cool waterholes in the 100-degree heat

I can barely contain the love of this iron cockring
of trusting faggots
faerie circle molten

Wolfboy heart
an opening timeless meadow
80 acres of sanctuary for fae ones
Our collective body
where we can sit and cry and fuck and share
and gather his magick seeds
—There are too many to count
falling from my open cupped hands
I feel like a big messy fruit
—And I am!
spilling my seeds and sweetness

Wolf Creek is forever

A   great   ripe   mango of joy
in my heart

HADRIAN AND ANTINOUS

Long ago (10 years at least) in a city by the sea
named for a saint called Francis
far upon the western shore
lived an emperor
in his own mind
who loved a boy
A boy who died too young

Like all lovers of that time
they were seen among the nightclubs
and the days
famous along the avenues
and carefree of the cafes
Their nights were made of love
and days of rest and longing

Fickle fate and the petulance of that plague
got a hold of the young boy and the emperor both
but it was the boy who slipped away first
leaving behind him the emperor
his friend
long to grieve and wander far

In sorrow, he deified the boy
and all across the empire
proclaimed his love and memory in statue
until all his subjects knew Dionysus
as a 25-year-old clubkid

A statue bronze erected atop Alamo Square
in the sun broke through the fog
And he there
a bronze angel
with tiny wings
A boy's shoulder blades
— he always was so thin—
shirtless bronze in low-rise levis, his boxers showing, a
   backwards baseball cap
his smile, and those eyes…

And on the corner of 16th and Mission
not far from the co-op market he priced fruit in
stands a copper boy

His skin was orange you know
— It's green now from the rain
He's got a tank top on
a pricing gun in hand hangs down close upon his waist

In the middle of Union Square
his arms ecstatic in the air
a dancing boy, his buttoned shirt undone
and head all shaven
Is it joy?
His eyes cast as to God —
or, asking perchance: *Eli, Eli, lama sabachthani?*

There's a Bufano, I've heard, of the boy in prayer
Some rich dowager has him in a garden
in Pacific Heights
among the hyacinth and narcissus

And a rumor wound round
that out among the lakes of Golden Gate Park
there'd been a boy of stone bathing like a heron in the reeds
They even said a statue stood straddling the toll plaza of the
   great bridge itself
his hands upon his bare hips, sturdy and strong

Most grand of all
stone images of the boy lined Columbus Avenue
from one end of it to the other
like some European Boulevard of centuries past
The thousand faces and poses of Pan they'd said
each one horned and nude
Each one a line of a dirge gone on too long
Too long
Too long
To love and lose
And long to long

For what are cities but graveyards
What is love but a funeral pyre
And lost love a stone

MY PERFECT ANDROGYNE

He hated being cute
wanted to be tough
pierced up and tattooed
leathered and bootblacked
with those big brown doggy eyes

He hated being cute
I assured him his body
was anything but—
that lithe, snake-like belly,
those athlete's legs
and soothing sisterly hands,
and his tiny male ass—
that handsome, unmistakably tough
cock
as hard and undiscriminating
as the policemen's billy clubs
that didn't want his HIV status
stopping traffic

I think of all the lives
it's just run over
unmistakably tough
and I think of all the goddesses we need
to hold us

Oh Mary, Mother of God
I never feel so close to you
than when I'm in his thin androgynous arms
under the gaze
of those doggy eyes

MELCHOR'S ASS

I love to be up Melchor's ass
It's my favorite place
Like a coffee shop
My flung cum like inspiration itself, a million poems, whole
   novels
Blasted up the boy's insides
You're well-read, boy

Give me a doubleshot, little Melchor begs in his hoarse boy's
   voice
And I write another song
My laptop, Melchor
Every sperm a journal entry recounting his boyness
My anal confessional
A dark, dank place where I spill my secrets
A rectal canyon in the hills —
No place I'd rather hike in and climb around
Melchor's ass should be a designated wilderness
Protected for posterity by government edict
No poaching my Melchor boy
And how much like eggs are his slack wrinkled balls shaking
   as I carve a new trail
And hack back the brush
All the birds are safe to sing here

Melchor drives a forklift
Stacks a warehouse full of pallets
After work we meet for coffee
Mochas and lattes
The sound of hot steam in our ears
Let's go to Melchor's and stay there all day
The door's rather tight
And the building is narrow
But the atmosphere is divine
With dimmed lights
And cave paintings on the walls
The music too is unrivaled
Melchor at full decibel
A shouting little punk star
Fuck me!

Ah to spend leisurely hours sipping him
The milk never running out, steamed, foamy and fresh

The boy is a handball court
A theater
A garage
A tunnel
A bridge
A river
A valley
A holy temple where I offer my relentless boyhood, my
  thanks
And all the humble poetry I can muster
I am only a man after all
And his asshole is god

IF THICH NHAT HANH WAS a FAG LIKE ME

"I think it pisses God off if you walk by the color purple in a field somewhere and don't notice it."
           Shug Avery in Alice Walker's The Color Purple

In just this moment
I will smoke a cigarette
forget about ulcers, lung cancer, and HIV

For just this once
I will walk through the Castro
with a smile on my face
and not because I'm happy
but in the service of love
which was what this was supposed to be about

In just this moment
I will tell a man he is handsome to his face
that his body is beautiful
forever young and strong
and I will not proposition him

In just this moment
I will be the Buddhist
I'd promised myself to be
when I was 17
drunk on Kerouac
and Wilder's graveyard answer
to who the hell understands:
– *the poets and the saints*
– *they do some*

For just this once
I will take one step
and remember that I am nothing but what I give
humble myself
before the grace and gift of being gay

In just this moment
I will squeeze a tear
one drop of honey
one flower am I
walking in a field of flowers

JESUS CHRIST, ST. SEBASTIAN, ETC., ETC.

Your body
  is a crucifixion
  and your arms look best that way
The hair in your armpits   finally flowing
    like lamenting   music

That bent rib you have is the spear in your side
    O, your tits
are like the madonna's tearful eyes
     round and soft   powerless and tender

The bold hairiness of your legs   is saying quite plainly
I WALKED THIS MOUNTAIN
I AM WILLING TO BE HERE
    Your feet are endurance
and   of course   sorrow

The firm softness of your buttocks
  is pressed   lightly
  against the hard wood
      like how it presses against me
I want to apologize to its innocence

Your back is finally stretched
    lightened of burden
Your hands are finally open and empty   nailed into
  submission
having dropped   what they held   like sleep
    no more to do, to shape

Your cock   elegantly erect
  curves like a finger   motioning forward
    into the darkness and thickness
     of its surrounding blooming-african violets
The hair on your inner thighs   like a   thin
  stand   of pines
along a tundric peninsula wide   and breathtaking
  as wilderness

Your face is asleep   or peacefully dead
    with a faint smile

The contrast of your dark hair   and pale olive skin
is as   assertively aesthetic
          as   calligraphy on white paper

Crown of thorns
                    — bite me
This cup will not pass
and I stand in the rain of your blood

It is the picadoros then
and your heart is plunged full of swords
The immaculate heart of Mary
Sorrowful and Glorious
Sweet Homosexual Junkie

MUIR PASS

Scattered and broken
in milelong slopes
of shattered scree
like an iron angel's tears
or his piss
splashing like rain turning to ice
in sharp and angular stone

These stone peaks
like weather-beaten faces
who wear their tears
as molten scars
and jagged fractures;
who cried
some long time ago
when the earth was hot, wet and alive

I come here to remember
And to fuck my way back

NIPPLES

Male
Naked

Nipples

Large and cinnamon
Like the guileless eyes of a child
for his chest is smooth and unblemished by the sun

His nipples are the most naked part of him
the most boyish
He is unself-conscious of them
in a way he could never be about his penis
or his ass

Let him move his hips
and press his cock into me
bounce about me with his balls
I watch the still, quiet place
The vault of heaven over-arching me
For he is weather
And the twin nipples
Are the moon and sun
testicles of day and night
a constellation engendering myths of gods

His nipples
don't betray the promise
Celestial bodies
Great Buddha eyes of Katmandu
All-seeing, penetrating and receptive all at once

Eyeballs I can kiss and lick
and make stand up with their backs in the air
like spiders

Let him fuck me then
His nipples are like my first toy
The mobile over the crib
when I was a baby on my back
and stupid

What then is my IQ and all my years of experience

and education
before the primal and infinite beauty of this
cumming boy's
hip-driven
groaning
halogen headlight
stretched-penis-skin pink
spherically imperfect
rose-budded brave assholes
out here in the open
leathery scrotal-textured
and semen-promising
rough-hewn
calloused
yet soft

cherry blossoms

falling

male
naked

Nipples

OUR LADY OF THE FINE TORSO

(An Ecstatic Vision of Marky Mark in Calvin Kleins, circa 1992)

I go on pilgrimage to worship at his feet
in a bus stop shelter
at Mission and Cortland Streets
Our Lady of Gannett Outdoor
enshrined
and praised by randy pilgrims before black plastic pews
She blesses all the buses that pass
which are troubles full of passengers
She fills my member with the spirit of God
She's an ecstatic vision in the bus grotto
and I drop my pants like crutches
— that is the teaching in why hers ride so low
I dance a desperate momentary dance
of sad whiteboy rap
as She drops blessed white roses of cum
into my lap

I spill my seeds like broken pockets of change
drop them among the fragments sharp of broken glass bottles
that pile up below her male perfection
like discarded profanities dropped from the mouths of the
　　destitute
who lurk here
I wait for the bus of troubles
with my number on it
I can hear it coming on the wires
as I kneel for her blessing
for her instruction
And I feel a serenity
as smooth and warm as his skin

which is blown apart by gunfire
rosebush thorns
that draw bloody lines across his skin racing
parallel as the lane markers on this street
running fast as speeding cars across his immaculate torso
And all the electric bus poles have lurched from their wires
and tear at the sky like knives
frustrated buses
stalled and hopeless as problems unsolvable

They gunned down a 13-year-old child
before your shrine
and in the driveby spray
you burst like lightning in shattering glass tears
...and all fall down

Our Lady
like an orgasm of giving up the ghost
just can't hold back the pain anymore
Let the white pigeons fly away
Blind us in bullet whiteness
Blind us with the vision of your creative gism
catapulted across the centuries and into the hands
of cops who beat their billyclubs like jackoff
over the shoulders of desperate youths

You are forever Our Lady of the Fine Torso
enshrined in the Mission Street grease and grime of my mind
a vision of raining glass and white roses
your skin torn in thorny lines
the children of the damned
murdered at your feet like martyrs
kneelers for the black plastic pews
where mothers say their rosaries
and wonder why their prayers, like their votes
just don't seem to count anymore
They sit and wait for buses full of angels that never come
and weep below your beauty

OUR LADY OF THE SHOWERS

He appeared
A vision in the showers of the YMCA
One bumpy blue vein
curving rakishly across his uncut cock

He must be a cad I thought

But he wasn't
He was a sweetheart and I was a slut
I guess I treated him like an object of beauty
though he'd been the Virgin Mary once
in a grotto
at the YMCA

I use that shower still
whenever I'm at the Y
think of what *could* grow at my feet

I have his water here to bathe me
whatever storm he came from
whatever promise he holds like spring
I stand here and try to feel it

He's rain
He just is
Once and forever
rain
And I wouldn't know love
if I fell in it
headfirst down the well
I wouldn't know it until my bones broke
like momma's water
me falling
in a hail of rain

I wouldn't know a blessing if it came
curving rakishly like a comet from the sky

I must be a cad

OUR LADY OF THE LOCKER ROOM

I first came upon her in the grottoes of steamrooms and
   saunas
She it was who was sweating with Christ's tears
 – and sometimes you could even hear *His* groans –
her power swinging from her waist
like a sensor
as she walked through the steam across the tile floors

Later, I'd find her in showers
peeking at me from out of the rain
Sometimes I'd ask for her phone number
Sometimes I'd make offerings
Sometimes there was darshan
Sometimes she blessed me
my tongue out as I genuflected to receive the host

Sometimes I just stared
She was fucking everyone in sight
Oh, what an active deity she was
busy comforting her children
busy giving to them
and letting them give to her
And she only asked them to play
She never asked them to suffer for her
 – *unless they were into that of course*

Sometimes she'd bless us with visions
Once, in a circle jerk in the steamroom, we all went off
   together –
Johnny sent forth a dozen narcissus; Corey a huge white
   chrysanthemum; Ben filled the air with a cloud of jasmine
   blossoms; and me, I ejaculated a thousand dandelion pods
   into the mist
And when I joyously laughed,
only bubbles emerged from my throat, but not a sound
Absolute silence
In the showers, all the drains were clogged with white rose
   petals
and there was a scent of chestnut trees in seed

On another occasion, I entered the sauna to find 4 men on
   their knees
And she was milking them

Cockcows, she whispered, dressed in the guise of a farmboy,
   naked but for overalls
I can still hear that music in the tin milk pails

They took a wrecking ball
to that old gym in time
and with it, she vanished
We wept, a temple in ruins, another god dead
echoing in the flash of her final vision —
the wrecking ball morphing into a giant scrotum, 2 low
   hangers swinging with joy —
I am Vishnu, creator and destroyer of worlds

For a long time there were but rumors of her appearances
And then, not 6 months ago,
I awoke at dusk to watch the day begin
And when the sun broke across the hills
my face was drenched in her cumshot
3 full shots
and an overpowering stench of bleach

HOW THE LION GOT ITS ROAR

I like it
when your asshole
grabs my cock
like a hand
saying:
"Daddy, Daddy,
…take me
to the zoo
where the wild animals are."

BONER POEM

There are many kinds of boners
not just the meaty ones in spades
Some people's hands have boners
— they can never be busy enough
Some people have ear boners
and they collect music and gossip
Those with god boners
hole up in gloryholes of confessionals
or sing out as choirs fuck them silly
Most people have success boners
and they chase the tight little ass of the American dream
fisting corporations for cash
and coming out with a handful of change

There are the future-directed boners
probing the unknown years ahead
shooting their wads without even knowing who they're
    fucking
And of course folks get boners for the past
Nostalgia
the same tired old fuck over and over again
I get these
tearing through the trousers of the present moment
My brain's got a great big boner for badboys
for someone I saw a long time ago
My little brain gets so excited it cums romantic dreams
in the badboy's general direction
And what a mess it makes!
leading to cumrags of therapy and self-help
Then I get a boner for solitude
and fuck myself into isolation
My feet get a boner for the hills
and I hike up and down the mountains
back and forth across the state
in and out of the wilderness
fickle with the friction of thoroughfares
humping the hills with the rhythm of running away

But not every boner that forces its way through the bare-
    threaded jockey shorts
of who we're pretending we are has an agenda
I do get great big heart-boners
for those I love

I cum right in my friend's faces
—even when they aren't boys!
I can't help it
and they smile as love drips from their chins
as they squirt right back at me
We swim together in the gooey seeds of love
You know something?
I just realized all my friends are assholes
Fuck them all!
Suck my dick, buddy ole pal!
We make a mess of love like children
Some people call us careless
but our balls ache without conditions
What do friends say they do together anyway?
They screw around
They fuck around
Socializing is masturbation
Jacking off with your friends
Spilling your seed where the soil makes flowers
which are nature's boners anyway

The earth has a boner for the sky, the sun and the moon
That's what the trees are saying so tall and firm
And the mountains
thrusting stone up
—and even the steel highrises and concrete towers of stiff
  rebar
Every person is a big boner
horny for love
standing erect
beautiful to look at
strong and swollen with rich veins of passion
wondrous to watch as they release the life that is in them
Blessed Boner beings all
Fountains of love
Shafts of light
Biological and Beautified Boners Forever and Flowing!

ODE to HIS BUTT

We were the same that day on the beach
the sun and I
staring at your butt

And on the bus ride home
I wanted to be that sun-dappled plastic seat
and hold those ripe mangoes

If your body was the universe
—which I suspect it might be—
your butt would be the sun and the moon both
and me an astronaut
longing to rocket between them
spend all my fuel

I think your butt is more like a couple of planets though
always cooler than the rest of you
goose-pimpled like the air at sunrise
big flat round stones in a garden
after rain

And the sun —
It's a tongue of light
and your butt is 2 cool pools of water
penetrated by and shimmering in a yellow star's ecstatic
   stoned laughter
I dive open-mouthed
not caring whether I drown

We're the same that way
the sun and I
We rise and explode
and do what we do
unconcerned with consequences

We think you're ripe

EVILDOERS

Imagine a world of young men
Frustrated
Unempowered
Vulnerable to manipulative, religious nutcases
Vulnerable to a bad idea about God
Vulnerable to a failure of imagination
— that breached levy that religion fills

But the truth is
God is what happens when people fuck
Even a Christian fundamentalist would agree,
though he'd need a temple of rationales to surround the
   concept

You don't buy it?
Well, I'm not here to proselytize
Let's bid for the boys
I'll meet your 16 virgins and raise you
3 uncut cocks and a tight boy's ass

But "sperm is cheap" says Edmund White

Plenty for everyone then

In a world of perceived scarcity —
— there is enough food
— there is enough medicine
— there is enough love
— and there's more than enough sperm

It's all in the systems of delivery

Walls of greed block the food and medicine
Religion blocks the sperm and love

Do the algebra and you get:
Greed+religion=poverty=powerlessness=violent young men

But in the grass roots of their balls
They are wealthy beyond measure

Wouldn't the algrebra work just as well in reverse?
Peaceful, tender young men, well-fucked and spent=personal,
   animal power=the wealth of joy and peace and truth and
   love=spirit, free of religion +
—well, who needs money?

We have sperm
Millionaires all

ODE to DJ

I'm in the mix, and the mix is in me

I don't really know him, but he knows me
Gets inside my deepest cell like DJ DNA
See he's got the key:
Double helix, rhythm, sound —
Deep House epiphany

And He,
He plays me

The night is his body, and the DJ, he's a gene
Can make down go up
And mix up all that's in between
He's the funk that through the green fuse drives the flower

Black light and dark, broken dirt of the night
DJ pushes me like green grass from the soil, born
And waving like a snake
Into the sky
Pops a flower or 2
Grows a goatee of twined bodies sexing in the night

And the freeway that arcs over these dancefloors
Busy bridges of sound changing lanes
He brings them all down
To spiral through the sex and the psychedelic psychology
Swimming in the green vines of his mulch and mix
Enwrapping me and rapturing
A symphony of who knows what and never heard again
These tunes of his are once upon a time
As are we all

And He,
He plays me

He's grown me into a tree
I'm a heaping pile of mashed potato cumulus clouds
Moved by his stormy, slippery hand
Mixing up the weather
—He makes me rain
He's windy, the sound of gravity and speed

And He,
He's moving through me

He's the chromosomic code that makes me hip-hop
Defines my everchanging form:
A blade of grass, a vine, a tree, a cloud-driven, weatherbeaten
symphony

He's the source and the sun
And the axis of the earth
— He makes it spin
And mixes you with me
In a congenital dance of ecstasy

And he —
He's a divine thing

So, when the night comes down like rain
There's a bass line splatter on the street
The world's a grease-gone gutter full of noise
Echoing his stormy message from the sky,
From the sea
From the river come back around
And come on back to me

It's in the mix
And the water like the music never ends

MILKY WAY

Beauty of your youth
how it spirals
Capricorn-acopia
Coiled like a snake
I don't know if it's getting ready to pounce
like a recoil
or just tightening
pulling itself inward

Maybe both at once

And I don't know whether the universe is expanding or
    contracting
Your asshole does one thing, your cock another
Gravity and fission

Infrequent as a comet
Still you orbit me
And you so into Saturn
I've seen rings of halos around your cock, your throat, your
    heart

You are like the Milky Way
the way you fling stars off the end of your long spidery limbs
Exploding nebulas of semen fill the void
and pull at my heart
Gravity and fission
At the center of you they say there's an enormous black hole
It doesn't sound like a gateway
But I'll take my chances

THE MOON

(One Night in the Mountains, Staring Stoned at the Moon)

Oh, what I see in the moon!
The man,
definitely 1930s
The woman,
with her look of surprised shock,
a curl of hair in her mouth
—No, it's a porn film!
She's about to take it in!
She's changed!
Oh, what other worlds in the keyhole of the moon!

There's a Hawaiian prince in full headgear,
the Napali coast behind him,
emerald mountains and surf
in black and white
He's not so different from the viceroy's son
in uniform and cap
with that colonial seal of authority behind him

And the smiling Jewish father
who died on TWA Flight 800 over Long Island
The shadows below his nose
his calm, contented smile
The perfect afternoon light on his half-portrait, half-profile
grinning-happiness-of-being-loved photo in a silver frame
I know children somewhere, and a wife, have lost their man
and he's on the piano now

Oh, the things I've seen in the moon!

The British in India with sari-ed throngs in the background
A maharishi and his disciples
U.S. Naval Officers
alone
with beautiful Hawaiian scenery behind them

A dog, with a spot on one eye
like the one in Little Rascals
at the front doorstep
with the newspaper in his mouth
And a little spotted black and white kitten in the flower bed

It's a baby dolphin
in the amniotic sac!

The moon

Over cities, forests, oceans, murders, and parades
The things she sees!
I can tell she plucks her eyebrows
So 1930s
And maybe that's just a microphone she seduces

She does shine in stagelights
with all that nightclub lounge drink-clinking black around her
She's a star!

But she isn't!—we all know she's a round rock

She's got sideburns now!
It's Phil Collins as a bald cherub!
Innocent and crooning
She's so full of herself
The little girl moon doing good
Little shape-shifting portal to the light beyond all the black

It's so choral, the way she sings
Rosy cheeks and chin cherubic
The moon's a little cherub with no wings
because there's science now
Little cherubs pulled by gravity through the time warps of
   space
Forces uncontrollable
Sex, greed, fear, and desire
The things she sees!
The things she must feel!
Pulling her around in earthly circles
She's a socialite in orbit!

"Help! Help!" she cries
wingless and spinning like a top
across the celestial black slate dance floor
patterned with a shattered strobe
"Help! Help!" she cries
begging that the earth and all of us
keep our safe distance

as we laugh:
Girl's scared of a carnival ride!

I throw out my arms
and something pulls me
like an anxious little child by the arm
And we dance swing, round and round
The moon and I
It's definitely 1930s
black and white
A photo
lost in time
An old phonograph with a scratchy song
We're little babies in each others arms
with big blue searching eyes

Oh the things I've seen in the moon
and the moon in me!

DRAG QUEEN DHARMA

A lotus flower
above the mud
her practice is her heels

PAN on TERRORISM

Pan has his arms crossed
And his brows knit
Appalled by the antics
Of sexless men
Feckless and fuckless

A paradise full of virgins
What crap
(As absurd as Christian monogamy)
The world is many things
And if it's fucking you're after
This is it, assholes

It's spelled out in genitals everywhere you turn

There are no virgins or whores in heaven
For those who've fucked and good
Know that paradise is nothing
The vanishing point of sexual release
Emptiness
Oblivion
A jewel proferred by the cumming Buddha

So get a clue, angry young men
The jewel is in your boxer shorts
It grows from out of your own mud
It's name is Prostate
And it is legion

Now put down your explosives
Drop your pants
And serve god and country

ODE to BUDDHA

Oh scantily dressed boygod
teach me your tantra
deliver me from the samsara of my bed

I've treated a thousand cocks
like lotus flowers
perching myself on them like a throne
But still I feel nothing

Teach me your tantra
look in my eyes

I'm cruising for you, Buddha
a man with something more to give

I say, if you meet the buddha in a nightclub
pick him up for chrissakes!

Sitting's getting me nowhere
I don't care about the one hand clapping
I'm tired of masturbation

Teach me your tantra
make me your mudra
steal my eyes

Call it the middle way
You're the kundalini kid
guiding it up the middle of me
your noble 8-inched path

Teach me your tantra
sing me your song
Fuck me right out of being
with your blessed dorje dong!

THE ARISTOCRACY OF THE SCROTUM

Languid it churns
Nonchalant
Even at moments of intense excitement,
while the penis makes an eager fool of itself,
the scrotum—heavy-lidded blue blood,
born to privilege—
yawns, sips, raises one eyebrow
The family jewels indeed

It's a constitutional monarchy
We moderns have no appreciation for its insouciance
Let them suck cock
it says dismissively
The scrotum is king
If it could smoke, it would

Secure in its power
Romulus and Remus
The holy twins of Gemini
As indolent as symbolism

Prince William and Prince Harry
I'll bet they've got real nice scrotums

EVANGELISM

Cum is like a bible
We shove at each other:
Here, look at my genes
Take my ancient story
Tell me it's the best
The truest
Tell me there is no other god but me

PSALMS FOR CENTAURS AND SATYRS

PAN

Oh, Pan
Even in this dehumanized high-tech tragedy
I see your image
Squeezing joy like aerosol whipcream out of us
and flinging your laughing cumbliss through the spring-
   loaded spouts
of Windex spraybottles
Teflon-tongued toad, penis-powered jackhammer gism germ,
   prefabricated python
pillage my private parts and publicize my pants

Oh Pan, o-pen u-pon these uppity shores
They tried to tell me you and the devil were one
at a time when that kind of distinction mattered
— Cloven-hoofed clubkid
pitied and parodied by populist pundits

The way you river-rush around
Oh adreneline angel
and blooddrunk bumblebee
Oh lymphatic lilliputian
and bile butterfly
You're my crazy cum-crane of a cock
and my assiduous asshole androgyne

Oh Pan, o-pen uh-pon
these poisoned penitentiaries of production
Drag my child-soul through the tight vagina
of growing old in an adult-deformed land
Drag it kicking, midwife magnificence

Oh Pan, o-pen
me!
Coax my kindness out of the highrised city
of competing cocks at sunrise of greed
skyscraping city   cumming rules and regulations
Coax me buttsex beautiful and bodacious out of the beehive
   of behavioral boroughs
Out of the putrid incandescence of irretrievable incarceration
in the pill-pandered prisons of pain
Wallop the crucified words castrated of imagery
and resurrect my ruminating fetus rife with randy reverie

Fuck me now, Pan
before I panic into pan-lingual pantheism of proselytizing
that carries you far from your name
Pillage me now, Pan, before I poem-pump
my personage into perfidy
and perpetual peroration

Pick me Pan
Pick my cherry-blossomed penis-powered
postpubescent prostate before its pilfered
Oh Pan,
Penis-prod me per diem
into the promised land of your pureed power

ELEGY for the CASTRO

A neighborhood is a body
But it's Picasso-esque at best
Sometimes I thought I was on its back
Or under its foot
Just inside the knee
Upon the hip

All I can really be sure of
Is that the Castro Theater —
Big pink neon minaret —
Was its cock
And not so much for where it was
Or how big it was
But for what spurted out of it
Like celluloid cum:
Yellow Brick Roads and Metropolises
Bette Davis retorts and Fellini's clownish cavalcades
All to the tune of a Wurlitzer
(A fun cock, a sublime, poetic cock indeed)

But the neighborhood around it
Wasn't as constant nor as inspired
It was like a Gulliver tied down by Lilliputians
He was a tired satyr, the Castro, when I met him in 1988
He still had balls, but he was bloodied and tired
We demonstrated for him weekly
Though with each new day they mounted more virulent
    campaigns
To tear our signs down
And it wasn't just ACT UP that gave the Castro its acne
But everything from poetry and performance to punk
    mayhem and music
And all things that made San Francisco great and free
And that's what being queer was and always will be:
    great and free

But I never blamed the Castro
Tied down in vanilla S&M by little people
I kept going back to the theater
To laugh and cry
Sucking off his true essence
Until they closed the donut shop,
Shaved the satyr's leg

First they made him wear shoes
Then they removed his hooves
And replaced them with tender feet
The better to match his dermabrasion and liposucted 6-pac
When they clipped his tail and closed down the last used
   bookstore
I left
Frankenstein the makeover
But I miss Frankenstein
The big forehead, the neck bolts and body hair
At least they've let his cock be
Though they've shaved his pubes

They've made him into a statue
So he can't embrace the young faggots in sweaty arms as he
   once did
But he holds out his hand
Which is better than any other American city can muster

You don't hate your parents
Because they get old and move to a golf course
Love never grows in the soil of disappointment
All things change, but nothing dies

So I return to the body of the father, the mother, the son
Ay, the holy ghost of my own lost randy youth
A sigh won't get me laid
But I've returned to the root
The cock of this body
The asshole of its auditorium
With its Buddha smack dab in the middle of the ceiling
Faded and dark
But laughing still
Like a prostate
A bubble and a dream

And today they showed *La Vie En Rose*
And I walked away spent
And filled both
Reminded and consoled
That all that lives is new
Is new
All that lives is new

VILLANELLE FOR A PANBOY

Is it possible to love a satyr?
The sex is good, but he won't linger
And will I see him later?

Empty as a moon-like crater
Weeping, I'm a hollow singer
Is it possible to love a satyr?

Intent he was upon my manly nadir
Will he plunge again his stinger?
And will I see him later?

Of my longing, he's the emancipator
The water and seed bringer
Is it possible to love a satyr?

To my every lustful pining does he cater
Of my body's cashdrawer he's the cha-chinger
And will I see him later?

Without him, I'm a sorry masturbator
Dreaming—why, he even had a cloven finger
Is it possible to love a satyr?
And will I see him later?

CRAB PANTOUM

Sorry crabs, things got tough and I got traditional values
– crucified 'em all

I know what I did
Took Reagan's advice about North Vietnam
God of retribution
Paved my crotch and painted parking stripes

Took Reagan's advice
Showered my revolutionary People's Park with rubber bullets
  and tear gas
Paved my crotch and painted parking stripes
paratrooping paranoid through the Crab Nebula

Showered my revolutionary People's Park with rubber bullets
  and tear gas
Quarantined my clothes like Japanese at Manzanar
Paratrooping paranoid through the Crab Nebula
Looking for a dry-cleaned philosophy that'll quell my itchy
  fears

Quarantined my clothes like Japanese at Manzanar
And now I'm scared of my shoes
Looking for a dry-cleaned philosophy that'll quell my itchy
  fears
Napalming my queer dick with Nazi skinhead medication

And now I'm scared of my shoes
I'm a xenophobe
Napalming my queer dick with Nazi skinhead medication
I don't want your poor huddled masses yearning

I'm a xenophobe
I got strict immigration policies
I don't want your poor huddled masses yearning
I'll kill all the firstborns like Passover

I got strict immigration policies
One of you's got the secret
I'll kill all the firstborns like Passover
Dead nits hanging on my hairs like messiahs on Golgotha

One of you's got the secret
We had to drop the bomb on Hiroshima to save American
  lives
Dead nits hanging on my hairs like messiahs on Golgotha
You seen one redwood you seen 'em all

We had to drop the bomb on Hiroshima to save American
  lives
God of retribution
You seen one redwood you seen 'em all
I know what I did   I know

ALAS, BABETTE THE COCKATIEL IS A COCKSUCKER

Oh, I have known men with the teeth of horses
but never have I been beak-blown
It will take some getting used to
Your mouth
all made of bone
makes me realize
my teeth are rows of hard-ons
And when we kiss
my dear beaked boner
our saliva
turns to fruit loops
and the milk runs down our chins

So we shall fete, Babette,
and better yet
dear prodigal pet
we shall perch you on our penises
where you'll do your bird-brained dance
like a clubkid
to the thump thump song
of your newfound homo lust
till our faerie wings flap with yours
and we lift off together
in the white-hot flash
of a birdsong slippery and sticky
as fruit loops
—and the milk will run down our chins

A NIGHTCLUB SOUTH OF MARKET

(Written after Allen Ginsberg's
"A Supermarket in California" upon his death.)

What thoughts I have of you tonight, Allen Ginsberg, for I walked through the deserted streets of North Beach musing on the Beats and despairing that I've arrived 30 years too late, looking still for the full moon hidden in the fog.

In my lonely fatigue, and wondering about love and connection, I ambled downtown and further still in the empty hours long after midnight, into a neon pulsating nightclub South of Market, dreaming of your enumerations! Wondering where the best minds, the best hearts, the best souls of my generation have gone.

Could they be here? And among such outfits! What lime green polyester and baggy pants dragging through the dust! Whole cliques with multicolored hair! A dance floor full of sweating gym queens in baseball caps and tight little shorts! Wispy-goateed waifs on Ecstasy! Young boys pierced and tattooed, so young and modern they've grown ancient and primitive, confounding time!—and you Allen, what's that smile on your face as you watch them? What magnificent imaginings of hard-cocked liberation and swinging scrotums, what thrills abound in the exploding Buddha realms of your mind, cock-full and cum-slippery, bursting with boys and men locked tongue-in-tongue as penis-joy is launched one upon the other.

I saw you, Allen Ginsberg, boyfriend-less, lonely old troll, leaning in the blacklight among the meek and muscle-less and eyeing the shirtless adonises, their gentle, thin lines of hair that swagger downward below their navels.

I heard you asking questions of each: Where do you scavenge such clothes? How much time do you spend at the gym? What are you trying to tell me with those green ink images dyed upon your skin? Are you my Angel?

I wandered in and out of the brilliant squirming mass of bodies following you, and followed in my imagination by Walt Whitman, James Broughton, and Antler, lonely ecstatic poets all.

We strode through the seething, spermy crowd together in our solitary fancy, tasting armpits, possessing every musty, hungry asshole, licking nipples and hairless flanks, feeling some boys calves resting on our shoulders as we roll together like the sea and its tides, and hearing each and every boy and man's orgasming whimpers and cries — poets of cock-play all.

Where are we going, Allen Ginsberg? The doors never close here, but you are leaving. Which way does your beard point tonight?
(I touch your books and touch myself, dreaming of our lonely odyssey in the nightclub and feel absurd.)
Will we walk all night through solitary streets? The eaves of warehouses add shade to moon shadow, lights out in houses, cafes, and stores, we'll both be lonely.
Will we stroll dreaming of the lost America of love, the lost youth of boyhood dreams of ecstatic unions, the elusive transmissions of teachings through cocks and male love as we pass the shattered windows of broken-into cars and heaps of homeless souls hiding from the wind?
Ah, dear father, graybeard, lonely old courage-teacher, clown and boy of song, what America do you leave behind and which do you look forward into? What reincarnated infant are you now, a baby of Dharma, born with its heart outside its body, struggling to breathe and longing to love. The Buddha said that an angry man will be born into anger, a quiet one into peace, and a man singing will be born into song.
Grant me now the strength and spirit to honor your soul with my own humble musical words, oh Bodhisattva, who I know has returned to teach us once more about love.

THE STAR SPANGLED BONER

Sing about the purple majesty of penises
Sing about the shiny sea of precum glistening on your shaft

Queers of America are beautiful
God done shed his grace on thee
In amber arcs of piss
so gallantly streaming
running like rivers from purple mountain majesty of cock
that I so proudly hail at every twilight's last gleaming

I sing for the fruited plane of existence
I find myself upon
Fruits and flutes everywhere
playing their liquid music
amplified by homo-lust
Hard homo cocks ready and song-singing ripe
as corn on the stalk
Heavy and thick
ready to be grabbed and husked
like the outstretched hand of a queer Uncle Sam
saying:
I WANT YOU!
—Suck my dick, Uncle Sam
I love your teeth

I'll suck your dick, America
And I'll lie down like the prairies
and rise like the Rockies
I'll cascade my cum lava
like Mt. St. Helens
Only, fuck me, America
like the road that rises to my summit
Fuck me
And let me fuck you
Oh fuck you, America
Let me gloriously unendingly fuck you
and make you a real man
A real home of the free and the brave
Cuz how can a man be free or brave
if he's never been penetrated?
Opened himself to another?

There is no bravery
nor freedom
in being only a fucker

God Bless America
And I am the blessing
I'm the great horned God
and I'm fucking horny

And this God's gonna shed his grace on you
and all your big United States
gathered together under your skin like muscle
Shed his grace 10 ccs at a time
Gonna drive it deep into your Grand Canyon
Gonna grab hard ahold of your Snake
River
Gonna drink your Rio Grande
I'm gonna run my teeth right along
The Blue Ridge Parkway
outta the Smoky Mountains
cuz I wanna smoke yours America

I wanna run my tongue along the perimeter of Lake Superior
shaped like your big-sack low-hanger balls
Oh, the bread basket of America
I wanna open my mouth
and swallow the whole fucking corn crop of Kansas

I wanna sit on Manhattan
I wanna wink at Queens across the river as I do it
I wanna be the sea for your Long Island

I'm gonna arouse this nation
with semen-song
I'm gonna get the whole state of Florida
to lift its southward bend
and point straight north
and live up to its legend
It's the fountain of youth, remember?
And I wanna swallow that fountain

Oh, let me sing how California looks like a big bent hard-on
my favorite kind
And I long to be Oregon
long for the cargo I know is coming up Hwy. 5

I wanna fill the empty asshole of the Great Basin
I'm gonna swell as red as the name of Colorado
and ride America buckin' like that cowboy on the license
    plates of Wyoming
Sucking your pioneering dick
is my manna-feast destiny

Oh Glory, Glory Holy-lluia
Stab me with your terrible swift sword
Union soldier
Only not so swift
Take your time
I wanna feel your grapes of wrath
stored like a harvest in your balls
hanging like a bunch of grapes before a Caesar

I'll whistle Dixie
And I'll spell that with a "CK"
while you invade me and put me in my place
Emancipate my manhood
Only I want no civility in this war

I wanna lick the jock strap that are your highways
crisscrossing this nation like woven thread
on a sweaty garment

I'll fall to my knees
faster even than your economy
and beg like the auto industry
for you to pump me full of investment tax credits
retrain my workers
and do it with leather, Daddy
Fill my tank with your gasoline
crude and thick

I wanna eat out your heavy industries
belching a smoke that I find divine
I'll lap up your toxic dumps
I'll join the military —
only let me shine all the marines' boots
and their various weapons with my tongue

Plymouth Rock is your fucking adam's apple
and I wanna suck on it
That's where I'll begin, too

And Oh, I will revel in thanksgiving
like the pilgrims
as I pull down the pants of your forests
and drive my tongue like progress
—like the railroad
right through any wildness you have in you

I'll blast my steam locomotive
belching its white-hot water all the way to California
where I'll dive right off the rocks of Big Sur
into the cumbliss of crashing white waves

I'm gonna stick my dick
right through the hole in the ozone
"Global boning" they'll call it
and the acid rain will turn white with seed

Oh Queer America the Beautiful
For spacious skies
Lay down honey
and look up into those skies
as I come down on you
like rainswollen clouds bursting
and fill you with the manhood
you've never been able to prove
Let me fill you with it
And let the gay soldiers fill all your trenches with cum
God done shed his grace on thee
In fact, God wants to pump his grace
slam his grace
groan with it
spit it with a thrust up your avenues
in Anytown, USA

I'm gonna cover you in my whiteness, America
whiter than the snow in North Dakota
or the salt flats of Utah
And it's gonna taste just as salty

Let the winter come
Let the snow fall
and cover you
Let every immigrant run urgently up the insides
of your drag Lady Liberty
like a randy cock

singing in its liquid white voice
crazed with lust for America —

Singing
with the sexy queerdom of choirs:

My country 'tis of thee
sweet land of sodomy
Of thee I sing…

L'ENVOI,
OR, PAGAN BENEDICTION

TIME HOLDS US GREEN AND DYING

We were green and young
Firm branched and budding
Our manhood flung

Through gardens and garages
Gym showers and alleyways
The kudzu of our desire

Quills full of ink with so much to say
Long scrawled stories across each other's chests
Graffitied rectums and gums — sex is a poem

Whole forests were lumbered for paper
Old towering growth felled
Like spent erections

Clear cut, or uncut
Like explorers, we sought harbors
And obstructionless passage

Fools, too roused we were
To let the risks curb our phallic enthusiasms
So many of us die green still

The cross and the sword
Saplings, shoots, and seedlings
The war for light, the shadows

We of the canopy
Icaran for Apollo's affection
Jack and the Beanstalk

We were green and young
And always will be
We are kudzu; we are trees

Trebor Healey (www.treborhealey.com) is the author of *Through It Came Bright Colors*, winner of both the 2004 Ferro-Grumley Award and the Violet Quill Award, and the short fiction collection *A Perfect Scar & Other Stories*. He has published poetry in more than 50 books, reviews, journals, and zines. Trebor lives in Los Angeles, where he has just completed his second novel, *Faun*.